The Gardens of Flora Baum

◆◆

Book Two

Towards a Greek Garden

Julia Budenz

Carpathia Press
Chelmsford, Mass., U.S.A.

Carpathia Press
7 Colonial Terrace
Chelmsford, Massachusetts 01824
U.S.A.

© 2011 by the Estate of Julia Budenz
All rights reserved.

Published by Carpathia Press. Except for brief passages quoted in a review, no part of this book may be reproduced by any mechanical, photographic, or electronic process without the written permission of the Estate of Julia Budenz. Address such requests to Carpathia Press, 7 Colonial Terrace, Chelmsford, MA 01824. Printed in the United States of America.

Library of Congress Cataloging-in-Publication Data has been applied for.

ISBN: 978-0-9849089-2-9 (softcover, bk. 2)

The Gardens of Flora Baum

II

The Gardens of Flora Baum

Book One: By the Tree of Life
   Part 1   Sum
   Part 2   The Path Approaching
   Part 3   Epiphany
   Part 4   The Waves Receding
   Part 5   Difference

Book Two: Towards a Greek Garden
   Part 1   The Program
   Part 2   Iliad
   Part 3   The History
   Part 4   Odyssey
   Part 5   The Diagram

Book Three: Rome
   Part 1   Urbiculture
   Part 2   Floralia
   Part 3   Umbrageous Vision

Book Four: Towards Farthest Thule
   Part 1   Lay of the Last Monk
   Part 2   Sibyl
   Part 3   Lyre, Harp, Violin

Book Five: By the Tree of Knowledge
   Part 1   By the Tree
   Part 2   The Tree of Knowledge
   Part 3   Knowledge
   Part 4   Of Knowledge by the Tree
   Part 5   Tree
   Part 6   Knowledge of the Tree
   Part 7   Of the Tree

BOOKS	PARTS	PARTS
Book One	5	
Book Two	5	10
Book Three	3	3
Book Four	3	
Book Five	7	10

Foreword

THIS IS A posthumous publication, but Julia Budenz had meticulously prepared her five-book poem and had overseen the process of digitization and proofing, and so it has the stamp of authorial approval. It rests on the author's typed version. Only the few pieces written within a week of her death on December 11, 2010, are from manuscript, and these are inserted at the points she indicated. They are "September" and "And January" (Book Three, pages 718–720, 722) and "How shall I say this?" (Book Five, page 570).

Her long poem addresses a wide range of readers, and she would have wished this first contact to be an unmediated one. So no attempt is made here to categorize, other than to indicate, as the poet did herself, that there is a different focus in each of the five books. In a short essay called "Query Re One's Work," which appeared online in the *Poetry Porch* in 1997, she said:

> The gardens are five, comprising the five books. The first garden is the garden of the holy; its book explores transcendence, is located partially in Eden, and draws upon imagery from the Bible and the liturgy. Its title, "By the Tree of Life," indicates that despite its strong center this book may be considered a Paradise Lost, as is suggested also by the names of its five parts: "Sum," "The Path Approaching," "Epiphany," "The Waves Receding," and "Difference."
>
> The second garden is the garden of the beautiful; its book contemplates the aesthetic, is situated partially in Greece, and makes use of Greek literature, mythology, and geography. This second book, which is called "Towards a Greek Garden," has a midpoint as well as a final destination and also consists of five parts, whose names intimate both the patterned centering and the linear progression: "The Program," "Iliad," "The History," "Odyssey," "The Diagram." Since Flora Baum reaches the Greek garden, the second book may be designated a Paradise Regained.
>
> The third garden is that of the true, specifically of academic

knowledge, of scholarship, of learning. Its book, entitled "Rome," uses material from Roman literature, history, and topography. This is the pivotal book in the design and development of the poem; its three parts — "Urbiculture," "Floralia," and "Umbrageous Vision" — mark not only a center which is both city and garden but also a difficult struggle to pass through pedantry to erudition and insight.

The fourth garden is that of the good and blooms with human relations. Its book, "Towards Farthest Thule," is set partly in Britain, finally in Shetland. As might be expected, it utilizes English and Scottish literature, folklore, and geography. The book begins with a long ballad, "The Lay of the Last Monk," continues with an epyllion called "Sibyl," and concludes with a sequence of lyrics, "Lyre, Harp, Violin."

The fifth and final garden is the garden of the whole. Its book, "By the Tree of Knowledge," is the philosophical book, the one most fully placed in Flora's native America but also situated in her native world, in her homeland the earth, in her home the universe. It is the book of the elm, rooted and reaching. It grounds itself not only in a meditation upon philosophy but also in social science and physical science, in culture and nature, in the microcosm and the mesocosm and the macrocosm, in the final paracosm, the final paradigm and paradise. It is the book which I will write if I can live long enough and become wise enough to do it. "O mihi tum longae maneat pars ultima vitae," I find myself crying out with Virgil, hoping to touch this great beginning or end or center or edge.

Although no critical assessment is offered here, it can be anticipated that, in due course, *The Gardens of Flora Baum* will find a place in the history of American literature once readers have had a chance to absorb its author's new and distinctive voice and to respond fully to it.

Julia's life and writing were intertwined and the following biographical sketch may prove helpful. She was the eldest daughter of Louis Budenz and Margaret Rodgers Budenz and had three sisters. She was born on May 23, 1934, in New York City. The first break in her life came in 1945 when her father renounced the Communist party and rejoined the Roman Catholic church. The family moved briefly to South Bend, Indiana, before returning to New York. The year 1956 marked Julia's graduation with an A.B. summa cum laude from the College of New Rochelle and also the beginning of the period she spent as an Ursuline nun. In 1962, she was awarded a Master of Arts degree at Catholic University and became an instructor in classics at the College of New Rochelle.

In 1966, after leaving the convent, she studied briefly at New York University in the spring and began graduate studies in comparative literature (Greek, Latin and English) at Harvard University in the fall. She graduated A.M. in 1972 and continued working towards a Ph.D. for a time, but the pull of scholarship in isolation became less compelling than the desire to create in the light of her scholarship and her vision. She began writing *The Gardens of Flora Baum* in about 1969 and received a fellowship at the Radcliffe Institute in 1974–75 for the purpose of developing it.

For the rest of her working life, she undertook paid employment with an eye always to the opportunities offered for the combination of scholarly facilities and leisure essential for her writing. Widener Library at Harvard University had the central place in her life that she speaks of in her poem. In 1972, she had begun working in Harvard's History of Science Department with I. Bernard Cohen and Anne Whitman on their new English translation of Isaac Newton's *Principia*, and, although she left Cambridge twice to teach classics — at Colby College in 1980–81 and at Berea College in 1987–88 — she was mainly engaged on History of Science Department projects until her retirement freed her to concentrate on her poetry. She suffered from ill health in her closing years and died of cancer at the age of seventy-six.

Parts of *The Gardens of Flora Baum* have been published previously in books and periodicals. *From the Gardens of Flora Baum*, Wesleyan University Press, Middletown, Connecticut, 1984, contained "The Fire Escape" and "The Sheen" (Book Two, pages 173–250), and *Carmina Carmentis*, Pivot Press, Brooklyn, New York, 2005, contained a sequence from "January" (Book Three, pages 635–673). Shorter pieces from *The Gardens of Flora Baum* were included in these edited books: *Anthology of Magazine Verse and Yearbook of American Poetry*, ed. Alan F. Pater, Monitor Book Company, Beverly Hills, California, 1980; *A Formal Feeling Comes: Poems in Form by Contemporary Women*, ed. Annie Finch, Story Line

Press, Brownsville, Oregon, 1994; *Catullus in English*, ed. Julia Haig Gaisser, Penguin Books, London, 2001; *Emily Lyle: The Persistent Scholar*, ed. Frances J. Fischer and Sigrid Rieuwerts, WVT Wissenschaftlicher Verlag Trier, Trier, 2007; *Petrarch & Dante*, ed. Zygmunt G. Baranski and Theodore J. Cachey, Jr., University of Notre Dame Press, Notre Dame, Indiana, 2009.

Other excerpts from the work appeared between 1971 and 2010 in the following periodicals: *Akros, American Arts Quarterly, The American Voice, Amphora, Arion, Bits, Bitterroot, Boston Review, Bunting Institute Newsletter, Chapman, Cloelia, Cosmos, Crazyhorse, The Cream City Review, Cross Currents, Epos, Four Quarters, La Fusta, Harvard Advocate, Harvard Review, Italian Americana, The Kenyon Review, Lines Review, The Lyric, Mati, NEeuropa, New England Classical Journal, North Stone Review, Notre Dame Review, Other Poetry, Persephone, Poet Lore, The Poetry Porch, Radcliffe Quarterly, Rhino, Scottish Literary Journal, Society of Fellows News* (American Academy in Rome), *The Society of Institute Fellows Newsletter* (The Bunting Institute of Radcliffe College), *Southwest Review, Sparrow, Studia Mystica, The Tennessee Quarterly, The Tennessee Review, Vergilius, The Wallace Stevens Journal, William and Mary Review*, and *YIP: Yale Italian Poetry*.

Very warm acknowledgement should be made in conclusion to those bodies that, through residencies, fellowships, visiting scholar appointments, and funding, gave support to this long-term poetic project. I shall instance with gratitude the American Academy in Rome, the Authors League, the Bellagio Study and Conference Center of the Rockefeller Foundation, the Djerassi Foundation, Harvard University's Departments of Comparative Literature and English, the National Endowment for the Arts, the Radcliffe Institute, and Yaddo.

EMILY LYLE
University of Edinburgh

Publisher's Note

WHEN JULIA BUDENZ began writing *The Gardens of Flora Baum* in about 1969, she prepared master sheets on a manual typewriter. By 2005 she had switched to a laptop computer, which provided digital files. The arduous task of scanning the older material (roughly 1,700 pages), processing it with optical-character-recognition software, and proofreading it was overseen by Emily Lyle. For questions that arise, readers should consult the original typescript included among Julia's papers, which have been placed on deposit in the Houghton Library, Harvard University.

Over the years Julia told friends the schedule she'd mapped out for herself, intending to finish *The Gardens of Flora Baum* in 2015, when she would have been 81. But in January 2008 she asked me to explore the idea of an "introductory edition" of the material written to that point, much of which had not yet appeared in print. She continued work on unfinished sections, mainly in Book Four and Book Five. By late 2010, with her health in sharp decline, she identified those places in the poem where she'd intended to insert further material.

In the last few months of her life she did make sure that the start and finish of every book were completed. She also discussed her preferences as to the layout and presentation of the books.

Layout and style. In preparing this set of five books for publication, my aim has been to follow the original typescript to the greatest extent possible. In most cases short titled pieces begin on a new page, or are run on with preceding pieces. The decision whether to center a title or place it flush left also follows the original. But a typewriter does not offer the stylistic variation possible in a typeset book, and we have varied heading styles to suggest the importance of each piece in the hierarchy implied by the table of contents of each book. The scheme varies somewhat from book to book.

The author's practice of having complete stanzas on a page, whenever possible, explains why some pages end short even though the piece continues on the next page. In the case of very long stanzas and other layout problems, we occasionally did break stanzas. This is indicated by the quaint device of a "catchword," set flush right at the bottom of the page. The catchword repeats the first word or two on the next page and tells the reader that the stanza has not ended yet. (To prevent anyone from mistaking a catchword for the second part of a broken line in the poem's meter, the catchword is printed in smaller type.) No catchwords were needed in Book One, but they do occur often in later books. On pages without a catchword, the page does end in a stanza break.

Occasionally the poem contains insertions that may appear to have been added by someone other than the author. One example is the use of "[sic]" in two places on page 79 of Book Two. Another is the inclusion of several footnotes in Book Five about a missing word or illegible date in a personal letter. There are a few other cases of partially bracketed dates at the tops of personal letters. All these insertions were made by Julia Budenz herself; she clearly intended them to be considered part of her poem.

Three asterisks (* * *) centered on a line denote a *lacuna*, or gap, where Julia had intended to write more material. On several occasions she commented that the asterisks could represent one stanza, one piece, or a long section of many pieces — there's no telling.

But the poem in five books appears to be at least 90 percent finished to her satisfaction. For the record, it contains about 303,700 words in 2,254 printed pages. The original typescript has 2,282 pages (owing to some differences in the locations of page breaks).

For advice and suggestions on specific issues during the preparation of these volumes, I am grateful to Virginia Furtwangler, Rebecca and Douglas Karo, Hope Mayo, Arthur Mortensen, Cynthia Thompson, and Frederick Turner. Without the monumental effort of Emily Lyle over many years, including repeated proofreading at various stages of production, this edition would not have been possible.

ROGER W. SINNOTT
Carpathia Press

Contents

Foreword   v
Publisher's Note   ix

Book Two: Towards a Greek Garden

Part One: The Program	3
Problems	5
Tree	5
To Hear the Harps of Heaven	6
Touching the Lyre	7
Relations	8
Similitude	9
Tempi	10
Equipoise	11
Mirroring	12
Transubstantiation	13
Round	14
November	15
Ride	16
Bells	17
Calendar	18
Darling Buds of May	19
A Filament	19
Scion	20
Candor	21
Cardinal	22
Sheen	24
Florale	25
Aition	26

Overlap	28
Post-Maian	29
Summer's Lease	31
Eve	31
Solstice	32
Magnificat	33
Sometime Too Hot	34
Aestivation	35
Indulgence	36
Animation	37
Minstrelsy	38
Adam	39
Roses of Shadow	40
Transfiguration	40
Assumption	41
Augustine	42
To	43
At	44
From	45
Labor Day	46
Weekday in Ordinary Time	48
Silver Fountains	49
Yellow Leaves	50
To Love That Well	50
Revolution	51
Cell	52
Portico	53
Temple	54
Studio	55
Choir	56
Rotation	57
That Time of Year	58
Late the Sweet Birds	59
Illumination	59
Text	60
Blue Monday	61
Ruins	62
Dominica	64

Migrants	65
Red Friday	66
Context	67
A Fulfilment	68
Intentions	69
Lineation	69
Trimming	70
Hierophanies	71
Rendition	72
Climates	73
Location	74
Rigamarole	75
Castle	76
Simulation	77
Theorems	78
The Poem Is as the Season	78
The Poem Is as the Year	79
Beech	80
Part Two: Iliad	81
Homère Lyricisé	83
Part Three: The History	85
A. Prorrhesis	87
1. Flora Baum's Curse	88
2. Flora Baum's Prayer	89
3. Flora Baum's Meditation	90
4. Flora Baum's Renunciation	91
5. Flora Baum's Vision	92
B. Flora Baum's Prophecy	93
1. December 21	94
2. After Compline, January 6	95
3. Persephone	96
4. Third Spring	97
1. Flora and the Maecenates	99
2. Breath	100
3. Native Daughter	101
4. Near the Charles	102

5. Limen Lumen	103
C. Flora and Cora	104
1. Flora Baum, Typist	105
2. Flora Baum, Filer	106
3. Flora Baum, Shelver	107
4. Flora Baum, Secretary	108
5. Flora Baum, Typed	109
1. Flora Baum, Factotum	110
2. Flora Baum, Employee	111
3. Flora Baum, Faineant	113
1. Hypothesis	114
2. Before Liftoff	115
3. Further	116
D. Nocturne	117
1. Seferis	118
2. Flora	119
3. Alles Epithymies	120
1. Flora Baum's Portrait . . .	121
2. Triptych . . .	122
3. Portrait of Cretogenes Zographos . . .	123
1. Anthe's Hand	124
2. Anthe's Dance	125
3. Stories of Sylvia Pezographos	126
4. What Then Is Love but Mourning . . .	128
5. Molpodora's Gift	129
E. Phegonaia	130
1. Interpretation	131
2. Epistemology	132
3. Question	133
4. Mythistorema	134
5. Prolegomena	135
1. June 21	136
2. Before Vespers, August 6	137
3. Demeter	138
4. Muse	139

F. Biennial	140
1. Theater	141
2. Theogamy	142
3. Diary of Flora Baum: Delphi, Bysios 7	143
4. Oracles	144
5. The Garden of Hephaestus	145
G. Mneme	146
Part Four: Odyssey	147
Proto-Pasch	149
Part Five: The Diagram	151
Dactylography	153
The Fire Escape	173
1. Sky	173
2. Tree	175
3. Season	176
4. Temple	176
5. Season	186
6. Tree	186
7. Sky	187
8. Tree	190
9. Season	191
10. Temple	194
11. Season	202
12. Tree	204
13. Sky	204
The Sheen	207
1. Troy	207
2. Ithaca	213
3. Delphi	221
4. Eleusis	228
5. Helicon	234

Book Two

Towards a Greek Garden

Part One

The Program

Problems

Tree

Dura in quercu invenire formam

The matter was hard.
You would feel it if you ran into the oak.

The idea was complex.
The truth of the tree depended on your question.

One day in a December
Of the year and of the mind

She came to the edge of the lawn
Without question, without running,

Only with eyes that crossed the iced grass, finding
A gray shape on a gray sky,

A gray body with black wings,
A strong base, a straight flight,

A skyscraper of cut glass
Scraping and cutting to painless pain,

Impact, answer, rising
April, spreading June.

To Hear the Harps of Heaven

She heard them. Skeptics doubted.
She was a skeptic. She heard the harps.

Especially since it was out of her way
And cold and made her late,

She should have said, when she had digressed
To where the oak designed the sky

Gathered about its robust central tune
And into the refinements of its chords

And raised about it as a hall
For the concert, a resonant frame

To take the sounds of many moments,
The many sounds of one moment,

The one sound of one moment,
The sound beyond many moments,

That she had erred from the earth,
Or she shouldn't have mentioned it at all.

Must the poem aspire to the condition
Of the short story, of the snapshot,

Of strangers' conversation overheard
In the bus station, on the airplane?

She overheard the harps play
When she watched the oak open the usual

Muffling curtain. That firm thunder,
That delicate lightning, that rich gray,

That subtle black, that steady white,
That shattering prism burst through.

Touching the Lyre

Here, in a land without laurels,
The pin oak is the tree of Apollo,

Not a maiden but the kouros himself,
Youthful, archaic, erect, smiling,

Or else it is the fine-stringed lyre.
She put out her hand. In the rain

She felt the shining vibration
Of columns on luminous hills

Above blue tideless, timeless sea.
The wet December grass gleamed greenishly.

Relations

Similitude

There was something unseen that was seen,
There was something unsaid that was said,
As when you find blue in purple
Or hear the chord about to be played.
It was like a question. It was a question
Of likeness. There was a barberry hedge
Like a sunset over an ocean. There was
A sunset over an ocean. It struck,
On the shore, a bronze equestrian seated
On bronze as on a wave. The brazen
Sea came close. The barberry hedge
Was coppered beyond the rocks.

Tempi

When the sunny cuneiform of the ginkgo
Displayed itself on sky-blue morning
Every which way
She read the slow historical script
Of temple, glacier, survival,
Faint in the permeating flash
Of the golden moment's half-awkward grace.

Equipoise

A ragged, barberry beauty
Confronted her in the October twilight.
She forgot November.
There had never been spring.
Or November and April coexisted,
Purple and pumpkin,
Cinder and glass,
Riband and shred,
Just before and just after.

Mirroring

With the final ochred foliage
She was bending over the pool.
She felt there was much to discover:
Movement, depth, the self, the sky.
She bent to a fishy stir.
She leaned to a muddy plumb.
She got as far as a surface
Gilded by unreflected leaves.

Transubstantiation

The tree is not a tree
Although its taut gray straightness
Renders a major pillar
And the stretches of its horizons
Sketch a flamboyant pyramid
And the russet rustle has the luster of illumination.
Although any healthy pin oak
On a lawn late in October
May demonstrate such accidents
Is marble Venus a woman
Or bronze Apollo one of the guys?

Round

Agnosticism and mysticism
Cohabit in one soul
Almost easily. When freedom and dark
Coincide in November at five
You walk home with thoughts on the floor of your mind
Stirring like kittenish leaves on the road.
As you spent your day at the file
Forcing those beige rectangular forms
Into zip-code order
Your place, your sacred space, your home
Was exterminated. In clouds of spray
The victor withdrew, relinquishing
The cooped-up fumes, some corpses perhaps,
Much filing. You'll spend your night
With spices, cereals, pots and pans,
Shifting them from the divan or bed,
Shifting your thoughts as if you returned
The leaves to their places in the trees,
Obscuring the arrangements of the stars.
The leaves circle on the road.
The roaches languish in their cracks.
Kittens have filled the branches and cannot
Back down. Tomorrow the sun will circle
Back up. You'll alphabetize the beige
Rectangular forms. You'll come home and sleep
In the dark, the divan being filed
Under *b*, while under the bed
Kitty paws at a moving sphere.
What blue moon
Slips by the trees?
What sun's sun
In central dark
Trumpeting light
Is circled by stars?

November

In sun-spattered autumn distances,
Where views are longer
And trees are smaller and finer,
Spare brilliancies more piercing,
Strewn ground more soft and sweet,
When the blue pines of September
And the rust pines of October,
Spurning their straw, turn verdant,
And roses flourish fresh in the ruins,
To finger larger harmonies
Is not being pretentious.
The virtuoso mockingbird
Long-throbs from the high, bare stage of the maple.
The gray-bound beech contains vast scores
Of measured green and bronze and gold.
You scan the leaves in their gatherings.

Ride

As silver apricots dropped
From the stinking ginkgo she flew
On the softly coppery feathers
Of the metasequoia out past the real,
Past where Daedalus feared for Icarus,
Out where the winged professor said
Ideas were at home. Dismounting,
She knocked on the azure door.
Her knuckles grew blue. She dropped
Among the smelly yellowish fruits.
Next time take the key,
They're a little deaf, the professor said.

Bells

There was something unheard that was heard.
An ignorant clash produced a song.
The trumpets and the oceans brayed
Together. Perhaps alloy
Was harmony. Brass tablets told
What happened. The carillonneur
Repeated it. The marble Cyprian
Sank below the whitest foam.
The bronze god turned green in the sea.
I can't put my finger on the pain,
But it tolls inside me.

Calendar

Darling Buds of May

A Filament

The sun-silk of the dangling strands
Of the sugar maples signs
Blue May. A metaphysic,
Not cold, not hot, of yellow and green
Perplexes prose, evades the phrase,
Precedes the thought as it precedes the leaves.

I'm tired of prose.
I'm tired of who did what,
Of what he did, of what I might
Have done. There is an absolute.
There is a moment in May.
There is an absolute moment in May.

Where the starry snow turned black
The starred magnolia gleams
Cloudlessly on the blue sheer.
A cardinal flits by forsythia,
Or there are red tulips and yellow jonquils,
Or there is a red and yellow tulip.

There are the subtle and the flagrant,
And the pink breeze is fragrant,
And something within is vagrant,
And something without is migrant,
Comes within. A filament
Of joy invades the ache.

Scion

Shall I remember where I was born?
I sing the dulcet hyacinth.

Spring was the sweep of exhaust
Through lifted windows; spring was a shift
In angle of glance of rays that rose
From pavements; spring came in a pot
On the fire escape. I sing

The rhythms of pigeons, the melodies of buses,
The sweetness of penny Hersheys in subway-station machines.

From its container on the slats
The blue hyacinth breathed
Into a sooty gust. Into a head
At the window swirled
Inklings of earth, intimations of air.

Candor

Our hawthorns have bigger thorns
Well bared in our colder winters.

Our hawthorns have bigger leaves
Well shading our hotter summers.

Our cedars are false;
Our stones haven't known the Romans.

We're shiny still. Let's fill our meters
With big new thoughts.

When the straight oaks are laden with gold
And earth blooms with bright bodies

Fondled by sun, philosophy
Must not dissolve. That icy mind

Pointed by lucubration in lengths
Of darkness must point still,

Probing the ever-edged, spearing
The evanescent. Sharpen the pencil.

It's so surprising when hawthorns whiten
Again with blossom. Snow-clotted boughs

Must be penetrable to the newest Thales. From near the garden
A siren pierces pearly May.

Cardinal

She is used to golden fingers.
There they are again
Harping on the tenth May sun.
The fangs of the hawthorn withdraw
Under petalous foam. She is clenching her teeth
And reaching for red Betelgeuse.

What is it? That's not the question. She knows what it is.
The big matutinal book is under her arm.
She tastes the song long played
On afternoon sunbeams. The white emergent stars
Clustering over the boughs perdure
Behind her eyes. To see, to have seen,
In the brightest night, on the laziest day,
At the most essential second, the emanation.

Where is it? That's harder. The seer
Is not the critic. Direction
Belongs to the judge. For which branch shades
The brightest phoebe call and which the answer?
Ubiquitous panpentametric quest
This is or ought to be for her tonight
When the sun drops from the forsythia.
Was it from the strings of her own heart
That the song got between her teeth
And onto the tip of her tongue? Or did she find
A brightness high on the giant's shoulder
Or under the arm of a star? Or is it true
That the moon and the nest are one?

Is it? A bright, crested bird
Alone could sing that song. But the hinge
Shrieks as she shoulders this door.
To step from essence to existence is to move
From the dewy lawn into the ocean. Is the moon
In the ocean, is that glittering path
The sun, is the star that sent that light
Sending it still? How stale is the spark
Flicked from Orion's gun before
The Constantinopolitan tumble?
The little bird likes her scapular perch,
Or is to claw the real to bite the dust?

If it could be, she thinks,
If it could be in her pulses,
If it could be in the pulp of her page,
Then it would be, that harping of stars,
That red song under the golden fingers.

Sheen

The cherry blossoms hurt her eyes.
They flourished so cherrily there, so fluffed
And flounced, so flourishingly pale,
Between the azure river and the lazule sky.

You are not prettiness, deity of May.
It is not the pretty that hurts, not nursery
Pink and blue which bear the staring.

If she indulged in little ecstasies
From violets in rain, from subtlest gold
Dripping from oaks in sun, they could
Enlarge. Her eyes enlarged.

Her mind enlarged. To try to find
Through the ever-busy buzz
Of the drive what the bee seeks,

To see and keep on seeing
Through the ever-spreading dust
Of the drive what the sun regards,

To catch, hold, and present
Through the ever-flowing fumes
Of the drive what the breeze offers,

Or their more, their human more:
This is worthy of May,
Of pink-cheeked May,
Of incandescence in the eyes.

Florale

As from a transcendent wistaria
Drooping down a constellation
A strange thought is scenting her brain,
A thought not new but alien.
Inhale: It can suffice.

A little frightened, a little lonely, a little consoled,
She walks on from that place where the wistaria thunders
Above the sheet lightning of the dogwood
And the flames of the red azalea.
May's sly violence finds itself inside one.

It could suffice. And every year
It did. The violet swell
Of cello cascading, the purest stream
Of white violin, the whirlpool of fiery
Trumpet encompassed her mind.

It was in her mind. That was
What could be enough.
If she had not leapt the constellations,
If she had not met a flaming friend
Above the empyrean, she had breathed

Purple, heard white, fingered
The reddest red. If it is in her mind,
If she can play the azalea, if she can touch
Transcendence only there, it can suffice.
It can if it must.

Aition

It was the causeless joy which she enjoyed,
As when rain lit the lilacs and their leaves
Into a quintessential vert and mauve.
The cause was not the rain and not the gleam
And not the taste of summer under spring.

The herring were kicking up their heels
Near the waterfall. After knocking loudly
The woodpecker popped into his spacious dwelling.
She observed all these things. She plunged
With the swimmers and soared above the rain.
It was not, surely, being which she enjoyed.
Being was good and evil;
Being was caused and causal;
Joy enjoyed a nonexistent cause. Her steps
Grew heavy around the puddles. Ahead
A little girl splashed through.
Her thought splashed through. Again
She streamed up the stream and winged up the slant of the rain.

A face. Was that causeless? A face which forced
Not the second glance or the third
But the fiftieth and the five hundredth.
And as their eyes swam they knew
The existence of their May faces differed
From that of their August thighs. Their happy
Pupils watched May into November.
Bloom, fruit, leaves, birds, fish
Could go; all good and ill
Could go; all cause could hibernate.
A scent of lilac swiftly flew
Along the snow. The slanting flakes
Were strewn like petals. Beyond was a lavender sun.

There was a lavender joy beyond all cause.
The cause did not exist and if it did
Impinge was never placed outside a brain
Soaked in the spring, lit by the lamps of May
Lifting luminophoric in the rain.

Overlap

When the lilacs began to rust
The unmoved mover began to move.
There was that space between May and June.

There were two things;
There were what was and what she loved —
One yellow, one blue.

The gold of being could not be denied.
It paid her way
Through the short passage.

It paved her way
Though there seemed to be gaps
Where she stepped when dazed by the blaze of azure.

She moved through the space. The laburnum
Started to glitter. She was moved.
And although she knew that her sky

Whirled on she clung to the pole
At the end of which she could see blue stretches
Past being. She heard a green cry.

Post-Maian

In a green month, far from all motors,
When the ecstatic lift of locust bloom had subsided
And the tulip trees had raised many cups of sun,

She ceased for a time from the long walking
And rested in the silence of the virgilias.
That was an enchanted quiet

Filled with the richness of the virgilias
Weighty for contemplation.
She drew in scent, shape, hue.

Snarling erupts in her shrine.
Wasps, profaning the rotted screens,
Have stung her thought. It will recover.

If she had thought the smooth trunks pewter,
The bright leaves greenest silk,
The flowers thick white edgings of pendent lace,

She would have midasized fresh life.
The bees knew that, the breeze revealed it,
The sun forgave it. The bees were at the blossoms,

The breeze on the blossoms, the sun in the blossoms,
A playing, dancing sun,
Laughing a white summer laugh

In ringlets, in the ruffles of white pinafores,
In sundrops among shades. Later, when she closed her eyes,
She saw the blooms as they were, not negative.

Swifts kissed loudly in the air;
Blue as a white-sailed bay, the jay
Sailed clarion on; the robin was at his song,

Lovingly at it; the mourning doves ooed and ahed
And whistled beigely off: movements like wind,
The breaths of being at rest.

The motors were not so far as she pretended.
She heard them on the road and in the sky and at the lawn.
If they were not breathing down her neck

She would think them far, if there were many greens,
The glittering greens of the pin oak,
The soft greens of the maple,

The greens of sun and the greens of shade,
The light green of the grass,
The deep green of the pines,

The precious precarious green of the elm.
The chainsaw rang; the yellow sawflakes splattered;
A blankness supervened from hole to heaven.

She knows the prose: the streets where green
Ginkgoes are a pallid yellow,
Yards of pushy ailanthus and cans,

Earthless blocks, posted and unposted bills.
She has known the foamy undulation
Of the crab under rough winds of May.

Standing on the sidewalk looking over the fence,
Sitting on the park bench looking over her shoulder,
How could she regard the virgilias, the yellowwoods?

White flakes descended from white heaven
Like seconds from white day.
White flakes descended from blue heaven,

And later, when she closed her eyes,
The petals were still white
And the month still green.

Summer's Lease

Eve

I cannot remember
The gray-green cooling
When the sun finished edging off.
It is more gray than green.
It was more green than gray.

When this was forest
The bird that sang before the sun
Was a forest bird.
This is forest after the sun
Though the robin in the dooryard does not dream

Of the green glade,
The sootless leaves,
The nursed children in the branches,
The strong smooth arms in the branches,
The gray wolf at the door.

Solstice

Some things don't have to be sought.
As she rushed ahead through the stifling breeze,
Taut with, sucked by, nose pointed straight toward
The necessary undesired goals,
From the sidelines, like a million minuscule bells,
Mellifluous despite the exuding trucks,
Came the sweet call of the linden.
Six times that day she was speeding heedlessly by;
Six times the summons wafted.

Locust trees bear the light, tossing scent of spring,
But lindens are heavy, deliciously heavy, with summer.
Spring is a walking, summer a sitting time.
The canvas chair, white bench, dry grass
Serves for pew, the tree for text
And tabernacle. She sat for an hour of now.
The monstrous ancient body loomed,
The tiny yellow blossoms bloomed,
Sprinklers twittered below and swifts above.

Communication did not fail.
In green skirts and yellow petticoats,
Shunning the circumlocutions of the roses
In a nearby bed, the million addressed her
With rustling of ruffles, melliferous humming,
Settling about bent elbows. Up went the trunk,
Heavy and light, grooved and ridged, one and two.
Each cyme rested and swayed,
Or, dulce, perfect, alive.

Magnificat

My soul doth qualify the word
Once known as yes.
The bowed catalpa proffers choice
White posies to the second of July.
Like the white chalices lined
With plum and gold, the candid sic
Opened: lobed, auricular, receptive.

Intoxicating, amethyst,
Chrysostomous, chrysousious,
The question, the invitation, the command
Transformed the ear. The answer thus
Was such and so.

Noon tumbles toward purple, pebbles
Fling shadows, the great things dwindle,
The name changes, the name
Remains, the thing slips.
The golden tree remains,
The rain tree haloed in gold,
Slender as Daphne in transformation.

Sometime Too Hot

Poetry is escape.
As summer is sweated away
Sharp sun and soggy air
Consort. A monster is bred.

Must I crouch within
Four peeling walls
Desiring nothing of life
But cross-ventilation?

A warrior is bred
And runs across the plate.
The monster falls from the rim.
The runner circles exulting.

If it is the monster that escapes
Who sings the song?
What if from the monster's corpse
Ten enemies rise?

If the scoundrel sits on the divan
Exhaling fire, the warrior turns,
Leaning, thrusting, dancing through the window,
Past red, past brown, into the mapled green.

Aestivation

The red summer afternoon
Hung over the brown lawn,
Pressed down on the gray road.

There it was.
You walked through it if you walked.
You sat in it if you sat.

You were ruddled if you were,
Like the old red bricks of your building.
You carried the bricks on your head.

While you sat there without motion
You saw green banners undulate
Where a blue breeze blew.

Indulgence

This won't do, they said.
You must tell how it feels to be a woman
In the summer of seventy-eight:
To drop a yellow egg into a tube.

I'll tell how it feels, she said,
To scuttle by a garden on your way to work
And drop the small blue nucleus of your soul
At a hedge for day care.

It cries when I leave it, and I say to it, Honey,
I can't take you into that place
To be slammed onto the copier. Rest here. Let the sunflower
Dust you with gold dust.

Animation

On the way home I'm on yellowish crutches.
My shoulders creak,
My hands crack,
My feet bump.
I can hardly bend to pick it up.

It is blue like purple asters in the grass
At their bluest, perfused with sky.

I fumble. I am a brassy machine
Squeaking in the shoulders,
Crackling at the hands,
Rusting around the feet.
I bow jerkily, reaching.

It is a juniper-blue-fleshed nut,
Small on the mowable lawn

But not mowed in, not cracked,
Not irrecoverable.
If I can get it. If I can just get it in.
There. Inserted. We fit.
We grow together. We flow along.

Then we look for something.
Then we look at something.

Minstrelsy

In Scheria the blind singer
Looked at Troy. From an unreal land
He looked at reality. The dreamy Phaeacians
Were delighted.

The visitor pulled his purple cloak
Across his face, hiding his eyes.
The singer saw the marigold,
The chrysopsis, the chrysanthemum,

Which elms were down,
What latest sugar maple by the road
Stood red-marked with R,
Which leaves hung brown from the middle of August,

Which dear voices murmured beyond mountains,
What fair face turned beyond oceans,
What soft hand hung motionless,
Which men were down.

The visitor groaned. The blind singer
Opened his eyes and sang what he saw:
The summers that were too short,
The summers that were too long.

Adam

There were plenty of leaves
In the green garden
Before the fall. Before they grayed

We gathered all the gold and rosy
Beauties into a sunset under the pine
Beside the gate through which they had strayed

Out to the novel, darkening world
Where I tipped your cooling lips
But with winter was afraid

To touch the rose between your buttocks,
To taste the honey between your thighs,
In the green-gray glade.

Roses of Shadow

Transfiguration

Monstrous globules of rain
Are slipping, slipping along under the wire,
Then plummet.

It is very dark this Sunday morning.
Only the rain is bright.
The barks of the trees and the habits of the bushes
Are transformed: The silvers are bronze,
The browns are black, the rising
Are falling. With the entrance of August the sun
Is falling, if not from percipience,
Yet in the mind, even as it slips
Back into noon, drawing up the waters.

As my mind goes sliding along
Will it get in under the wire?
Then arise?

Assumption

In the middle of August,
At the bottom of an inversion,
With the rising of the dewpoint

And the brightening of the fruits —
Neat orange packages on mountain ash,
Crimson parcels on the sumac,

Rosying of twisted tags
On that weed, the tree of heaven —
And the barbarous rosying of the barberry foliage,

Babbling of autumn in heat,
As the green rosettes of civilized privet
Predicted the distant roses

Which laze here in florid senility
Over the deep green hedge,
Not quite evergreen, that will purple

When the long sounds have long ceased —
The lawnmowers and the cicadas —
With the short sounds of a few dry leaves

Underfoot now as the goldenrod
Gilds weedy August
And heavy hydrangeas droop,

It is possible to be taken
Upward and not merely,
As the Greeks believe, to sleep.

Augustine

Descendite ut ascendatis

The blue was up as August coolly ended
And people said: We smell the falling fall
Twirling gently from heaven. The white or purple
Butterflies are caterpillars now
Hanging on the virgilias and the wistarias.

One wild aster weakly twinkled by the road.
In it, as she passed, she saw the sky.
The sky glittered deeply, not of the savage stars,
Of itself, heart-rending serenity, sheen of the morning.
In it she saw what she felt in herself when she saw.

If she looked up, what else could she do? The sky
Always transfixed her eyes and her eyes the sky
With desire with the scent of one split sassafras leaf
That lay like blood on the sidewalk waiting for ages
Of transformation to show if the search was up.

To

There is a search going on
Through the gardens and out past the hills.
Do you think she will last? Will she find

That precise line of the mountain
Which is a dance,

That sure texture of the tulip tree
Which vibrates strings,

A swaying of the sedge
Like moist brushstrokes,

That exact shade of the sky:
The supreme stain?

She thinks the rose may be
At the portico's end. In the mind
There is something going on.

At

It seems to be the mind
That sees this great September elm.

Even though the eyes widen and the sinews stretch
And the breath deepens and the pulse becomes

Melodic, it is the mind
That, finally, finds.

A particle of beauty is beauty.
The gold oval floats in afternoon.

Lines and lines, fine, flaring, flung
Up and out, and twining up and in,

And twisting out and up, and flung;
The bangles swinging, swaying, summer-green,

Late-summer-green, old-green, in sun
A sun-new green, sun-fresh, a green like spring,

And sun-new gold, a gold like sun;
Ascending masses, rhythmic mass, refined

Solidity, unstirring trunk
With stirring foils can reach the watching mind.

From

That turn and turn of a head
Whose one turn must be cast.
The casting.

Involvements of the rose
When one curve meets the grain.
The carving.

A swirling in the breeze
Along the stone beneath
The chisel.

Labor Day

Bread and roses.
Who'll buy my roses?
I'm unemployed.

From the corner of Green and Pleasant,
Where the green is seedy ailanthus
And the pleasure a sleep on the sidewalk,
You pass the small paved lot and reach the red-brick building
With an unmarked door. You pass the door,
And the next is marked: Do not enter. Then
The building's edge. So back you go
And in you go, in the absence of prohibition,
Your head afloat. Within all is afloat:
Long lines of light in the ceiling;
The green geometry of desks;
The pleasant, patient employed
In their slow, unfathomable dance;
Instructions in five languages,
Unintelligible;
The unemployed waiting.

The pink lady floats down:
You can try, can't you?
You can fill it out, can't you?
You can't find out any other way?
The green lady floats up:
And now their coffee break.
The man is hearty: My last check.
I start to work next Tuesday.
The gray lady is encircled by a triple mantra:
As of July 29 . . . the regulations . . . only thirty weeks.
It's her thirty-first. The lacy lady
Floats back and forth with her rosy sores.
The gray linoleum plane below
Circles about the spaced rose squares.
That's what happened last week.
That's what happens next week.

Who'll buy my roses?
Can't sell my roses.
Can't sell myself.

Weekday in Ordinary Time

Feasts are out of fashion.
After right Pentecostal red
The eternal green is nearly unbroken
Till purple December.
Thus the old mother is renewed.
Rejuvenated, the scarlet woman
Walks through the years.
Here we are together,
Babble the parishioners and kiss.

Ordinary roses, red,
Nod by the ordinary fence.

I have stolen your feasts.
I have stolen your golden gowns
And recut them to fit.
I have set up your smoking perfumes
And sent up your glowing resonancies.
You thought you could keep them stored,
But I have made them mine,
Plucking them from your rejected hoard
For my workshop, museum, and shrine.

Silver Fountains

The perfect pears emerge on the perfect tree,
Glass-blown, pear-shaped pears, all bright,
Set in their setting of leaves. And rosy spheres
Glow on the crabapple boughs before blue heaven.

What ripening hue or tint or shade
Seeps through the silver-dusted plums?
Blue-rose-violet orbs are hung in green,
Deep-dyed-lavender eggs of a potency.

The mountain ashes are weighed down with scarlet.
Rosy fists clench on the cucumber tree.
Flashy autumn begins to flash.
And those brilliant roses are old.

Can I admit infection to the rose?
Can I admit rouge to the cheek?
Shall I admit a jubilation
Of blue tinged with crimson?

Yellow Leaves

To Love That Well

Like gray squirrels your eyes
Romp sun-tailed up the branches
In tune. Your hand throbs, bowing
The strings — the great contrabass of the bole,
Relentless cellos along the boughs,
Violin shimmer in the leaves — in touch
With the tempo of the elm from brown largo
To the presto of the diamonds near the sky.
Accelerando, diminuendo, con brio,
This vast taper tapers into green flame.
You know it all: the sureness of the trunk,
The push of the branches, the abandon of the leaves.
You know the mighty gush of the trunk,
The rivers of the boughs, the leafy showers.
The branching is the beauty — this branching is beauty —
You cry, and then the sun
Enters a quivering verdurous cluster.
You cry dimension, direction, ascent, and then
The downpour of the trunk
And in a green cascade
The flickering bits of golden foam.

Revolution

The elm's patch of citron luminosity
Is seven yellow leaves of light
Gleaming in yet-green September.

The names stay the same —
The green, the yellow,
The rose, the cello —
But then the yellow was turning green.
The order changes.

This is ripeness: the predicate is the subject.
The merry horses prance on their poles.
In the middle stands the dappled tulip tree.

Cell

In the monastery of the mind
The elm and I are alone
Under panes of sky.
Here are the streaked trunk
And the twisting limbs
And the old, dry, jagged leaves.
Here is the immense effort
Of motionless motion.
The monk sits watching.
The lines become a complexity,
A complication, an implication,
The many and the one.
On the very blue the very green
Translucinates
And the sun-fraught gold is the gold-caught sun.

Portico

After an hour of seeing nothing
I went away. Later, passing,
I glanced between columns. That snap
Of space and time, catching
One brown ponderous horizontal bough
Suspending emeralds, thousands,
Flittering, glittering,
Flowing, glowing,
Streaming, gleaming,
Flashing, splashing,
Showered sheen splendor.

Temple

Be sober now and calm.
Look at reality.
There are no emeralds here, no gold,
No diamonds near the sky. The sky
Is far away. Here is a tree,
Old and grand and sheen. And sheen:
Here is a temple for the mind.
Here is the place where that beyond the real
Is seen in the real. Here the lined leaves
Are verdant pages and the long lines of the boughs
Read back to the sky.

Studio

The delineation
Rises in clear air.
The people at the margin striding home from work
Are not shown.
Even at five p.m. the elm is edged
By the sweet clarity of September.
The pencil rubs along the bark of the trunk,
Lunges out the branches,
And dithers among the leaves.
That is the sketch. In the etching
People stride at the edge.

Choir

This is not damp, cold stone.
Mingling with shapely shadow the sun
Slips into the tapered ovals of the green and yellow lights,
Slides through arch upon arching arch,
Slants against the gray, white, and orange of the pillar.

Three, five, eleven, twenty
Branches of beauty rise and extend

In massive lightness, stationary wandering,
Tumultuous balance, throbbing calm,

Rhyming silence, intricate simplicity,
Figures, figure, forms, form.

There are no images here,
No angels on the corbels, no demons over the door,
No mother, no father, no son, no flaming dove,
Only the pigeons, the bark-colored squirrels, the sparrows,
Only one flying dragon spewing green fire to the south.

From the south shadow grows.
Behind the branches of beauty beauty

Stands, behind the forms the form
Spreads, out of the boughs the figure

Glimmers, lifts, seeps through eyes
Into a waiting, wintry psalm.

No bell rings in the tower.
Traffic surrounds the lawn.
Only, among white clouds, the six o'clock sun
Tolls the hold and release, the fused and defused,
The trough and crest, and celebrates the elm.

Rotation

She passed late golden roses,
The honeying virgilia,
The green and yellow motley of the tulip tree.

The elm was her pole.
It was most open, most closed,
Most to be chosen, most to be circled, most to be seen.

The elm was her pole.
It centered the messy horizon.
She could almost dance on the lawn.

The elm grew out of her sphere,
Thrusting, groping, wrestling into the sky,
Pouring, prodding, probing into the ground.

Among late sunbeams the elm was pole,
Foucault pendulum, sundial, clock.
As she watched the earth turned.

That Time of Year

It is still green. The yellow
Is still decoration, not of a season
But of one crown, a few gold baubles
In green tresses, a few gray hairs,
A sprig of the mellow.

The green veils flow,
Revealing that pleasant attraction of earth,
Revealing the breezes, revealing the sun,
In dangle, in stillness and stir,
In outer glitter and inner glow.

The lush fall is unthinned.
The ever pending pendulous drops
Here float, here hang, here undulate.
There they are tousled, there they are tossed.
The lamps are undimmed.

She never quite mastered the branches,
But they will survive the white shadow
Swinging through darkness. The easier leaves
Whispering all their sunny syllables
Leave before the world blanches.

The elm is old
Like the organ with the controlled roar,
The lion with the masterful leap,
That human body, tall and lithe,
With tousled hair, silver for gold.

Late the Sweet Birds

Illumination

> To be blue,
> There must be no questions.
>
> Wallace Stevens.

The text is in the center,
Line for line and word for word,
Minding its p's and q's
Like a green-gold lawn with every blade
Sharply alight, all smooth, and skied with blue.

Through the gate you see on the borders untamed roses,
Sea roses wild as the ocean, grizzlies
Feeding on wood-wild honey, bearskinned ascetics
Feeding on waste-wild honey, stepping
Into the red sea, into the blue-green flood.

What do you do with the brown-leaved elm
In green September? What do you do
With the red mastectomy, purple stroke?
What do you say if his hemorrhoids bloom
And her vaginal discharge oozes?
What do you say of the indigo wings
That never reach the winter-green south?

Selective scattering produces blue.
Shall we move to the black-skied moon?
Shall we put a black border on every page?

Text

Was prose the core and poetry the slough,
The book in bed after the nine-to-five,
Dinner, the dishes, the bills, the telephone calls,
Or was a sabbath center of the week
With winds here and there and lights off and on in the elm?
The bluest morning glory sets in purple.
The purple rose of sharon sets in blue.

Blue Monday

I've found a paying job again, you see.
My work, my oeuvre, my opus is a fringe,
A lacy edging on the tablecloth
Below the bread and meat. I feel a tinge

Of green on the cheek, of jaundice in the eye,
A flush of rosy anger to the east
And to the west the blackest melancholy,
Reaching my guildered hand to the golden feast.

Ruins

I.

It was May in old England
As we set out from Helmsley
Over the footpaths and the stiles

Through the motorless green undulations
With blosmen and with briddes roune
While thrushes called and swallows gathered,

Cows turned their heads and sheep looked up,
Clustered beeches leaved softly,
And the river whispered.

Out in this green country
In one greenest dale
Gray storied arches sang from lawns: Rievaulx:

A ghostly elegance of solid stone,
Where drifts of white-robed answering
Echoed in sun.

II.

It is September in New England.
It is Saturday, but the dust will stay on the floor.
Outside, August has been swept away.

In the fragrance of the afternoon
Scarlet stars are lustering
On skies of a Massachusetts blue.

The tuneless robins flick away,
But the sugar maples have begun to sing.
The songs are orange

With every half tone and quarter tone
From primrose to vermilion. Among the rests
Of green a period has begun:

The spreading of the red carpet,
The scattering of golden coins,
But first the bright dying.

III.

It is not sad to see
Beauty that was, that will be, that is:
The fallen, the falling, the fall.

It is not sad to see
The perfection of imperfection,
To do the undone, to make the unmade.

Dominica

She worked all Sunday.
She made a bronze man sinewy as an elm
With a laugh in his bronze throat
And a bronze strength in his thigh.
She made a woman whose soft cheek and breast,
Whose masterly flick of the wrist,
Shaped and shimmered through marble.
She made an Arab boy in lindenwood
And the lashes of his longing eyes
And the fine force of his ankles.
She worked in joy.

Migrants

The yellow-green birds in the birch
Were like yellow-green leaves.
We named them "fall" from the days
In which they were ours.
They moved from summer to summer.

They swept into the common hackberry up the path
And spent the weekend among the witches' brooms,
Fitting a yellow-green spell upon the green dome,
Setting it with twinkles and flutters,
Filling it with rustling and checking,
Suffusing it with flittings and gleamings
In a flawless orchestration. We filled ourselves
From this painting, this sculpture, this architecture, this stage,
This play, this dance, this symphony, this cosmos.

We wondered less at their whence
And imminent whither
(Labrador? Paraná?)
Than why the vibrant
Pattern was our satisfaction.

Red Friday

Friday is a red-letter day,
Ferial-festal, when tamed birds
Can fly, feral, away.

The honeylocusts, an hour ago,
Gold-fingered the breeze
Pianissimo.

Our fingers move like pigeons' heads,
But only our fingertips count
As they peck at the alphabet seeds.

It's merely seven more hours till reddest five.
Let's seek the true, the good, the beautiful
Before we starve.

We tap at the letters and spell
Ftarlusee, egvoiold,
Bheoarurtiibfluel.

We tap the sun across the sky.
We flip the seconds through the file.
Our fingers fly.

Context

If you step back you see
The rich red sleeves of the robe,
The white linen towel on the rack,
The white leaded panes by the desk.
The candle is unneeded.

If you step close you look out the window.
The white swans on the blue of the stream,
The white sheep on the green of the mound,
The green tree on the white and blue of the sky
Make May.

Fresh is that Flemish May.
Fresh is that scarlet robe.
Fresh are the unfoxed pages of the open book.
You note perhaps what the cardinal taps:
The yellowish ugly central skull.

A Fulfilment

Is there a bell that chimes
Through gray like this sugar maple?
This is shape and color
Too subtle and too flagrant
For paint, for metaphor, for any sharing
Of the shocked, solemn rapture.

Not the flaming flagrance of Florida
Or the subtlety of an April dawn
But an unstoppered vial of essence of October
At this half-temperate latitude, on this gray noon,
At this remove from the sun and from the ocean and from the river,
Grounds the most vaporous inhalation.

If I should sing the round of very red to very yellow,
The freshest remnants of pale green,
If I should mention the irregular regularity
Of a great soft bright sphere,
What would it matter to the people rushing to lunch?
I'm late from lunch. I back away.

Will this give some shape to life,
Give it a little color, this crystal, this dome,
Not rose, not peach, not apricot,
Not lime, not lemon, cinnabar perhaps
On a chromatic scale, as I back off toward the gray file
Under an unquestionable blue?

Intentions

Lineation

She wanted to run in long lines like the railroad lines running across the prairie,
She wanted to run across the prairie, to skim the mountains, to leap the canyons,
She thought she could fling her lines along the landscapes from sea to shining sea,
She thought she could fling them into the air above the native buildings of Chicago, of Manhattan,
She could float them from an empty seven forty-seven as she lunged from window to window watching the map,
She could ribbon the gulfs, the bayous, the Appalachians, the Rockies, the Great Salt Lake, the great fresh lakes, the Mississippi, the Rio Grande, the golden bridge, the raised torch.
It was nineteen seventy-eight, it was November, the trees had dwindled,
The American autumn had fizzled, only the Old World beeches were bronze and gold,
She was caught in a rocky corner behind the dry stone wall, behind the sticky brush,
She was stuck in the brush of the suburb with its short streets.

Trimming

She wanted to clip the hedges.
She wanted to mow the lawns.
She wanted to hammer the rock
Into a guardian for the fountain.
Under his calm hands
Benignity would flow.
Everything would be smooth
Except the water gushing like life.

Hierophanies

She wanted to tell her tale.
The sky spoke to her once and once the hammering Jehovah
   and once the sweet Jesus with sad brown eyes
And once the anointed victor, the living Christ, leaning from
   above the heavens, reaching to her with fire,
And Esse glistening crystalline far over sunrise and Scire like
   scarlet sunset around the bend
And once Zeus raining the golden petals with which she
   trembled,
And once she was shot up, up, and up the glimmering
   redwood,
And once she was caught in the lovely lingering tentacles of
   the elm.

Rendition

She wanted, in a butterscotch light,
To paint the afternoon. She esteemed
That afternoon, that light, the point
Where she met them halfway down the road.
She cherished, also, the diction
Of the pigments, the syntax of the strokes,
And the blue-green pool which she added to the hour.

Climates

It's clouding over in Massachusetts,
It's clearing up in Florida.
She found herself like Janus on Cape Fear,
Thinking of night-white tints of snow,
Thinking of green-winged, green-songed sunrise,
Thinking of the rugged arms
Of someone with well-pressed trousers and polished shoes.

Location

She wanted to know if the late rays
Of copper and lavender flowers in shaggy November gardens
Shone their muted penetrant gleams
There in neat bunches among the shags
Or here in the penetralia of attention
Or over here in attuned bowed strings
Or there, far over there, beyond the drums, the sunset, and the winter.

Rigamarole

She wanted to think that it mattered
That among universal circlings,
On a cog in the big procedure,
Near rocks assaulted by fists
Of puppets flung by lines
From cogs beyond, her hands
Shaped a castle in the sands
And she watered it with ocean
And watched it stick. Its motion
Seemed like growth. The signs
Began to weaken in the mists
Breathed ahead by the besieger
Among senescent gurglings
Before the atoms scattered.

Castle

She wanted silence and air:
Salvation from the grunts and grimy breath
Of the unremitting assailants of her windows.
Never live near a red light.
Over and over it angers the motors
Like bulls. As the deer longs for streams
So urban flesh doth lust to hear and breathe,
And so the urban spirit yearns
For atmospheres that carry tunes.
Here comes the wind siffling in the oak leaves.
There goes the mournful horn of the north.
She made a castle in the November air.
She played the harmonies of her melodies there.
The willow danced by the window like a maiden with long golden hair.

Simulation

She wanted the unreal to be real.
She wanted the page to prove
Her syllables were the barberry leaves
That wrote a demonstration saying
They were drops of beauty
As the lake drops were of sky.
The barberry leaves were of sky:
Fragments of sunrise,
Sparklings of noon,
Embers of November day-down,
Particles of orange moon,
In whole harmonies as of stars.

Theorems

The Poem Is as the Season

It's hard to go out searching for trees.
They're no longer gold.
You're walking on glass.
When you look up you're slapped in the face.
Diamonds over the beech make your eyes water.

It has happened before. It's winter. There's nothing
To say. The new snow is the same
Old virgin snow, the same old maid,
Soft, white, with diamonds in her ears
And on her fingers, clinging to the muscular beech.

The Poem Is as the Year

Due to [sic] the atmosphere of Venus
You can't see more than a mile,
But now one can detect
Old gravity's weak waves,
And we need minor not major poets.

That's where we are in nineteen seventy-eight.
That's how we are dated.
That's how we'll be annotated.
There was a splendid autumn in New England,
But the snow came early.

Poems must be prosaic
Prior to [sic] nineteen seventy-nine.
But then, the forecaster says,
Venus will step from the beech at the end of the mile.
Warm waves will pulse through your cold fingers.

Beech

Librum respicere fagum

By an insite force the book goes on
In a straight line towards its end
Or endlessness. It is a point
On a line or a segment of a line.
It is moving forward.

By the force of the form it turns
And turns and turns around the tree.
The gravity of the beauty of the beech
Makes it face the massive matter gravely,
Playing the moon.

Part Two

Iliad

Homère Lyricisé

Anger. The faces turned. The lyre
Twanged. Anger is a thing
To be sung by deity, felt
By Achilles Peleiades. Swift
Fingers ran down the string.

Shifting ceased in the hall, all
Muted but the groan of Aegean
Waves, the moan of winds,
Curs crunching in a corner, the fire
Leaping in the center, the lyre.

The singer moaned. That hellish will
Without any measure caused
Achaeans torment, sent
To the death-god in multitudes strong souls
Of heroic men. He paused.

But the men themselves were being made
The prey of dogs and all
The birds, and Zeus was fulfilling
His plan. A shudder shook the note
And the scrivener's hand that wrote.

This was done and is sung from the day when first
Two men stood apart in hate.
How bitter the tune! The one,
Agamemnon Atrides, king of men,
And the other, Achilles the great.

Part Three

The History

Prorrhesis

I will see
What sprouts from rock:
What god-sown olive,
What god-made circlet of bay,
What god-spoken phonemes of beech or oak,
What god.

Flora Baum's Curse

Holy oak, summon the sky and the thunder
Against the men who will cut you from me. Armed
The guardians of the garden come too swiftly
Fell in intention.

Gold-tasseled tree, when all the rosy feathers
Had fanned and you were aureoled in the day-red
I sprang into the dawn with you and around you
Danced with immortals.

Green-pinioned bole, eagle of trees, reaching
The watchet sky, in meridian summer stillness
Poised and unmoving I sat at your root awaiting
Fructification.

Gray-tissued boughs, where was the crimson splendor
Cresting the sun-red west, where were the ruddled
Rustlings on musky beams under sweet-brushing
Breezes of evening?

Naked oak, gaunt and unshivering
Betwixt dim glitter in the cyaneous sky
And chilly earth, I leaned against your straightness
Out of the wind-whip.

Holy oak, invoke the sky for the thunder —
A voice before the void, a shouted-by-heaven
Witnessing: Guards, her life lives in this life.
She is a dryad.

Flora Baum's Prayer

Watch me, watchet sky. The pompous wardens of this yard,
Sparing my oak, have tried to inch me out
As long leaves darken while acorns scale
The branchlets. At the corner of a leaf
Within a great green egg of gall I curl
Trusting in you, blue serpent, to circle ever
Head to tail around the garden girding
My birth.

Flora Baum's Meditation

Coils of air have throttled the sky,
I thought in a blustery dusk
As the dragon blew.

Darker and darker it grew.
O my titanic oak,
What do you hold in your atlas arms?
Where is the high god serene over meadows of May?
Where is the high god, the father, vociferating the thunder
As long shapes slither through long green jungles
Of June? Where is voluptuous rain on July deserts?

Crouching in darkness I feel the dragon around me.
Twice he has lifted me; twice from his fangs
I scrambled up the ladder of the branches
And sat seeing over the leaves,
Over the hill, over the garden, over the wall, over the world,
Into the sky. The third time must I see
Over the sky? Is this that higher dark?
I push my eyes open against the enfolding blank.

The dragon, son of earth,
In earth's service, has swallowed the sky;
My tight cocoon is the silk
Of his heavenly mouth;
The wise worm must be killed
By those who will eat from the tree;
The tree must be devoured
By those who will fly;
I thought in the icy night.

My hand is patting the dragon's wing,
Seeking the merest sky, the bluest heaven.
Heaven, earth's consort, is earth's son.

Flora Baum's Renunciation

My tree, their tree, however dealt,
You are, once touched, forever felt
Within that curve: a pole
And lightning on the rebound and Prometheus
Just reconciled with Jove. Theirs can now glow
Into transparency, and mine
Flame lightly into the admiring eye.
An oak remains, and a sky.

Flora Baum's Vision

I.

All desire am I
For the infinite sky.
I wait in my binding clay
For the bloom of day.

I raise my hands to the rains,
To the rays of the sun.
Draw me along your lanes
To the endless one.

Lift me quickly on high
To the limitless light.
Rescue me from this night.
Let me touch the sky.

II.

Great bronze tripods lie here and there on the soil,
And barefooted priests are sleeping on the ground.
It is a dawn late in November. The cold
Has crawled over the mountain and sprawled in the valley.

The sun is just stretching a finger over the ridge
That bounds the sky. Through the pass and into the plain
Trudges a dusty heifer with human eyes.
I know that this place is a place I have never known.

In the sun the priests arise, the tripods arise;
Priestesses, doves, a holy grove appear.
What is the oracle? What is the meaning? I see
The speaking leaves of the chryselephantine beech.

Flora Baum's Prophecy

In an axil of an oak
I found a red, red flower
Smaller than a raindrop.

Gold tassels toss in the May rain.

The oak is a giant,
The oak is Briareos,
The red fluff smaller than a drop of blood.

Gold tassels toss in the May rain.

Gather, my friends,
Be glad and rejoice with me
At my ruby-ribboned cryptic prize.

Gold tassels toss in the May rain.

Rejoice at an auspice of acorn?
Be glad at a token of oak?
At a promise of polished plank?

Gold tassels toss in the May rain.

Not at a portent of acorn,
Not at an omen of oak,
Not at a promise. Behold:

Gold tassels toss in the May rain.

When promises plummet
And planks collapse,
A flower will have been found.

Gold tassels toss in the May rain.

December 21

Who can read the calendar of the mind?
What are its seasons?
April may trail after May.
June can presage December.

How long are the days?
How long is an hour?
How far is the sun?
And how many moons

Preach to the tides?
What are the texts?
Blessed are they that believe
And have not seen.

What are the watches?
What are the nights of the mind?

After Compline, January 6

You are the candle. The candle is out.
The light is wisdom. The light is gone.
The song is beauty, and I do not know
How to sing it. Wisps of incense float

Faintly through the pale between a distant vault
And the dim stones of the aisle where someone is lying
Rib to rock. For many hours we called.
You came brilliant in mist.

Come! Come! What hoarse cries crack?
Did you ever come? Who came? Come back!
Return in sun! The stained glass with a jerk
Of a tasseled cord drops open to the black.

I wonder who is standing in this dark.
I wonder who is singing from this rock.

Persephone

I know nothing here
Except that the streets are lined with headless
Elms it's dark it's cold the elms

Are their own tombstones my special
Section of earth is the bed of
Death sometimes I sleep sometimes

I walk through the cemetery of the elms remembering
Death feeling within me
I am immortal I feel my feet

On flowering mountains I feel my wanting
The millions of suns in the boughs of the olives
And in the burning waters kissed by sky

Third Spring

Dear old dragon,
Now that you are young anew,
Where will you take me clinging
To the sinew and subtlety of your soft blue neck?

Winds in sun winnow dust
From winter windowsills. Up! Out!
Won't we go far! This pilgrimage
Fiddles the moon, laughs along the galaxies,
Hurtles through the hedges of the universe. Stars
Prick my heart.

How thorny, how thick do you judge the hedges? Will our scratches
Bloody the summit? But around my ivoried bower
Privets twinkle into green rosettes. Big
Books on my shelves, big pillows on my windowseat
Suffice. I'll dine and live. The snake
Will fizzle in his buttery juice, and in my ears
The hiss of his slipping soul will figure less
Than the breath of balloons half blown.

Before our eyes float all the gay balloons
Of childhood, all the miraculous gas balloons
That went to heaven, alas, terrestrial loss,
From chubby fingers on bright afternoons
And in brave nights from skeletal fire escapes.

Now it is night. The floating fullest moon,
Orange and equinoctial, is remythologized
For our approach. Over the lovely floods
We'll pass in extravagant pasch
Though holding is hard and steering is mystery,
Managed, calculated, blind.

The moon is moving over the elm,
Your chin is resting on the sill,
My cheek is resting on your hair,
My pillows are plopping over the floor.

Now can we fly? Can I hold on? In our first two tries
We were so reckless in our rocketing
And then knew gravity.

Flora and the Maecenates

The splendid glass of their life
Outclimbed the whispering city,
Beginning in the midst. She began

In mist, she strolled in rain
Where April azaleas floated
In violet glisten. Soon

She would soar, tilt, and turn
Near the vertical glass, turning
A million eyes into pictures

Of a horizontal world. Not
Like a flower free in the rain
Would she soar. They would put her up.

Breath

That noon she knew the air was hot, moist wool.
The sun was a blast furnace blasting away
In the wool-white, satin-blue sky.
On a strip of tanned grass between
The concrete sidewalk and the asphalt road
A sugar maple was dying. No room to root.
She walked, she breathed, haltingly, without rhythm.
No room for breath in this wet desert.

In the dying tree,
Very high,
A bud,
A rose,
A rose-touched bird,
A rose-breasted grosbeak was dawning
In waves of sweet light and light motion.
A rhythm was dawning.

Native Daughter

Beyond the beady department stores,
Beyond the grunting trucks,
She sang under auburn fringes of elms
And maples' crimson lace
And maples' silken green dangles.

Crest rivaled crest, and a bright red flash
Matched bright splashes of blue
Where the cardinal called from the left and the jay from the right.

She sang of olives and laurels.
She sang with the nightingale.
She knew the ring of Apollo's golden voice,
She saw Athene's silver eyes,
She watched young Core spring from the soil.

Couldn't she hear in the trees
The song of the silver maple's son,
The tale of the maize maiden?

Near the Charles

By night the streetlights in this civilized river
Flicker, long flames,
As if candles were set in the river's bed.

In my city's river a fire
Quivers by night and by day —
An uncivil flame,

Hostile to the daily rowers,
Inimical to streetlamps,
A candle of Greece burning in Trojan Scamander.

Limen Lumen

Beyond the green lengths of the lawn,
Within the curve of the drive,
Before the red-brown shingles of the gabled house

Hover huge droplets of light,
Not white, not pink, something
Neither and both, between and transcendent,
Resting restless in the air.

The moment before —
Not only before the magnolia floats
Over the threshold of bloom —
Is the fullest, holding

Remembrance of every April of every year
Perfected through every February's patience,
Through every impatient March,
And blended with that prescience (dilating the eyes

And the brain behind) of the explosion
Of bud into image,
Image into song.

Flora and Cora

When it was May and she a flower
She barely saw the bloom
That made an opal of the earth. She reached for the sun,
Gold key to the sky. Let the sky now
Draw her up.

When in November a yellow rose
Shone on the oaken lid
Of the earth like a sunlet, she reached for the golden knob,
The leaves swung wide, rich Pluto
Pulled her down.

Persephone somewhere goes under in June
And comes up through the cave of October,
As oaks are burning to panel brown doors for the earth
And the sun dims for New England's
Proserpine.

Flora Baum, Typist

The daily Antigone trails
From a sun's world into the granite tomb
For that rendezvous with the machine.

Punctuation is hardest to efface. What retractation
Tames the comma into the period? O,
Fear the chalky tumulus, the cavernous lacuna.

I took gods for lovers in the nests of valleys
And for friends on the horns of hills.

What quotations in what parentheses or brackets
Leap the long void? What red
Rubrical ribbons fix the transitions?

She becomes a bent body
Balancing on a ball,
The end of a question.

Flora Baum, Filer

Fellow-filers of the world,
Come, let us worship the machine.

Fingers climb the walls of the cards
In servitude to the curved and angled gift
Shipped upon a time
Out of the economic East.

I blink. I shift.
How shall I hold up a head
Clenched in the crabby pincers
Of the inexorable alphabet,
A brain squeezed like the blessed martyr,
Margaret Clitherow, pressed for not pleading?

A clamped brain faintly throbs somewhere above, up there,
Up above the bloated feet that tread the wooden water,
Up above rilled fingers that move on like the legs
Of headless chickens and the hearts of split frogs,
Up above fishy eyes
Hooked to each line.

We eat three meals a day,
Pay our taxes, waste
Little leisure, wait
For an acronymed redeemer.

Veni ad salvandum nos, deus ex machina.
Come and save us, divine machine.

Flora Baum, Shelver

At the core of swirling universes
Lurks a granite cave.
There I stand eight hours a day
With a chain on my brain.

My name is Tantalus. I handle
Bolted books containing food
Locked from my hunger. The savor faintly
Tickles my starvation, but the key is time.

These shackles free others, they counsel. I confess,
A wave, a petty particle of my brain
Breaks into the glorious whirl sometimes,
Sometimes I steal the key.

Flora Baum, Secretary

This is the secret I keep:
I left the house
And gave you only my ears
And my eyes and my hands,

And my brain slid through the cylinder
And slipped out thin as dough well rolled,
Flat as the sheet
Drained through the ancient wringer and the antiquated mangle.

Flora Baum, Typed

She thought she might be a tree
Not estranged from the sky:

Perhaps a gangling ginkgo
Rescued from ice,

Perhaps a whimsical birch
Vying with snow,

Perhaps a linden in June
Enrapturing bees,

Perhaps a pagoda tree soaring
Lightly over July.

Someone thought she was a block of wood
To be cut with his name.

Flora Baum, Factotum

There is a gold like the sun that glows in November.
Lanterns may tumble from countless trees yet aureoles dazzle
    from beeches.
Am I a beech? Am I a tree?
Who has stolen my gold?
I am a pair of ears and a pair of hands.
Watch me quiver in the mist.

Who is the man or beast that eats my fruit?
My ears are floating like leaves in the fog.
My fruit has fallen like autumn rain into the swampy mouth
Of one who speaks to the sky,
Whose teeth have ground.

What is the muscle or bone that has thrown at me
Rocks and rocks of words?
My hands hang on a pulpy trunk
Numbed into night. And only the hands remain
To flitter in the whiffs of wind.

Suppose I were an auditory Argus.
Suppose I were a centibrachiate god.
I am a pair of ears and a pair of hands.
The putative rest is pelted or devoured.
I am a servant
Of the servants of mammon.

Flora Baum, Employee

I.

When we arise in the sunset will we wisp into the West
Stretching long fingers ever to the mirrored fingers of light
Touching the sun as it rounds again on the sepulchers of our days
Dropping the ashes through half-lit edges of morning

Or whirl away with the earth through the limits of night
Outstripping the spinning below us splitting the vast
Last blackened barrier with our arrowed hands
And streak to meet the onrushing East?

II.

Back down here where we machinate it is less that we are lead
In belly and in breast, and it is less
That from the leaden chest the iron arms
Can clack and clatter on, and that the head

Once dried and glassed
Can top a tool
(With engine elsewhere).
It is more that it will last.

III.

It lasts. It is the hours. On the new earth
The hours will dwindle and the week will wither
Into a day on which, shoulder to shoulder
With steel and calculation, we will not serve.

I think that it will be synergizing.

The lamb will lie down with the lion,
The hills flow honey and milk,
The man take his turn with the machine —
His short, short turn.

IV.

Yes, had I been a man I would have married
Earth, and we would live among our children
Working our works, and with our feet well grounded
Would entertain the planets and the stars.

The flowers are fair,
The trees are tall,
The sky is sapphire,
Below my beloved.

V.

We all have revolutions. As I roll
I seep through the granite cracks
In dying from time to time.
It is my commandment to myself,

It is my covenant with a super-sky
Which once beat down like a swan,
Which once bent down like a swan,
Swathing in flaming wings of light. It is aetherizing.

Flora Baum, Faineant

She was as grave as a jovial moon,
But she pulled herself free of planet, of sky,
Of god, for a year of perigesis
Beyond her stars, if shirking

Something, seeking something more:
As acorns grow and eaglets soar,
To pierce the edge of our spherical core,
Be light, mercurial, unworking.

Hypothesis

Protean dragon, ever one,
I'm holding on.
But what if by the time we are up
Our time should be up,
Before we clutch our contingency sample,
Before we snatch our picture for simple
Transmission? Unknown, we will know;
The inertia of flight will deliver us whither we go.

Reptile, butterfly, blue pegasus, blue air,
Far beyond the cosmos lies a garden of fire. There
Without the shadow of smoke
Burns a lighted oak
Beside a flaming spring.
All this you will ring
While I see, sip, and sing.

All this you have taught me, master.
No disaster
Will star us if we start a little faster.

Before Liftoff

I.

What great gulf gapes for us
Below Olympian aether? Snake, arise!
Within Greek skies lies aether's fire,
Higher than air. My airy snake, there is my burning.

Standing on tiptoe in Tempe, among the cool planetrees
Of Tempe, among the soft willows,
I'll long like a laurel for sky and fire.
I'll pile no Pelions on Ossa. If rocks will not reach

The rarest peaks, I'll poise in the subtlest valley,
Wave to the winding highway, pray to the sinuous river.
If the Hellenic land opens on the inner heaven,
I'll saddle my dragon in Greece.

II.

Domestic Zeus is serpentine,
Smooth as the oil of the olive oozing around our hearts.
The cave is cool. The dancers stamp,
The cymbals tingle the stars.
The cave is rough. The baby is soft.
Shepherds feel at home. Here we are at home. The cave is heaven.

Or does the aetherial equal the chthonian
Only in beginning
On the ground?

Shake your scales, lethargic monster,
Spark and spiral, try.
Blue air, blue fire, fly.

Further

Star of consciousness and passion,
Magnet of quintessential yearning,
Burning tree,
Candle,
I was a moth
Rushing out of the cold spaces of the night.
At purest noon,
Pale, unseen, the shade will see nothing.
Moths come and go.
Men blanch, leaves blush, at dying. It is fall
Around the flaming oak.

Nocturne

I knew the white face of the night.
    I felt the black hair
Meander under the curve of my hand.
    That was night's stroke
Slowly flowing over my shoulder.
    That was the kiss.
I knew the length of the night upon me.
    I felt the black waves.

Seferis

You went before I came.
I couldn't shake your hand
In Emerson Hall. I didn't turn
And whisper as you crossed Syntagma Square.

I stand under your sun.
I sleep under your trees.
I dance upon the rusty rocks.
I hold your rose. I meet you on this shore.

Flora

Maybe not yet the rose
But sun-ray-ribboned
Winter witchhazel curled against the snow
Bewitched me. With a stick

I wrote on ice: I am
In essence a question
Of desire. And with a sun
I flower and I melt.

Alles Epithymies

Like ancient bodies of immortals that have not aged
And they raised them with ecstasy to the shimmering temple
With roses in their garlands and in their sandals jasmine —
So stand the other desires that have raged
In the imagination only and on the mountain
Above the air perch undying and simple.

Flora Baum's Portrait

By Armenios Hellenas Callitechnes

She saw herself on his canvas. Her Byzantine eyes,
Frescoed by him, saw what he saw. Her mouth
From his tesserae sang his songs in a furnace of fire

Among the oily flames. She knew she was not
Autumnal in a fall that she knew. The canvas was not
The stained glass of October in Massachusetts

Nor she like a rubied red maple in Craigie Street's haven
Of frame and clapboard and shingle and lawn and hedge
Or the subtle citron and mauve of a Brattle Street ash

Contemplating the brattle, nor like that exuberant
Orange-red-orange sugar maple by Clay Pit Pond
Or an ambered umbered elm on a Belmont hill,

But Narcissus staring at the ruddy waters of Van
And Echo muffled in snows of Ararat.

Triptych

With Flora Baum and Armenios Hellenas Callitechnes

Are we both here? Hellas — to me
Olympus, Parnassus, Helicon — held
Your first steps. I thirst for Greek that is Greek
To me (numbing my tongue, rushing

Through my ears like a thunderous mountain stream
Through a valley in winter, trickling along
My mind like a brook over rock when aging
Tithonus clicks through August); to you,

First milk, old wine. Art for you
Is laurel, aureole, splendid exchange
Of light for light; to me, the star
Whose lucent arrow, dispatched before

The centuries, only last night grazed
The bark of the ever leafless elm.
Does Greece, to me ethereal soaring
Into sunrise, to you perhaps lie west?

Portrait of Cretogenes Zographos
By Flora Baum

There is much white here;
It is the snow of New England all around you.
My brush was white with snow,

With not knowing. You shook it off,
Striding over seas of ice,
Flaming as red and yellow and blue

As an island whose sky and saffron sun
Fuse with the blood that pulses young
In a world gone hoary.

Anthe's Hand

In that moment I knew she turned her hand.
The Sahara laughed

In a splash of fountains. Saskatchewan glowed
With the gold of the rose

That climbed through blanched December. A god
Fondled New York.

In that moment I knew my fingers tapped
Nothing of magic.

Anthe's Dance

We sat on the bank by Eildon Tree
    And the grass was so green and the hill so smooth
That I thought I would rest there forever, but she
    Suddenly stood and began to move

Beyond the hawthorn whitening there,
    Beyond the grassy tent of the hill,
Right through the flap, beyond the air,
    Beyond the parting of heaven and hell,

Along the third road, past the river of blood,
    Into a velvet land with skies
Domed by the arch of her arms. The bud
    Of a thorn tree opened behind her eyes.

Stories of Sylvia Pezographos

1. Sylvia's Prose

It filled my eyes and filled
My lungs and flesh; I felt
Through my sinews the classical dance,
The ephebe of friezes
Carved pure and perfect,
Distant and within.

2. Sylvia's Cities

Rain fell through the pages
And over the gray of the streets
And between the trees of the park
And the blades of the grass,
The still blades of the mower,
The blades of the mind.

3. Sylvia's Ocean

The ambulance pulled off.
The tide came on.
The child was crying by the tide.

4. Sylvia's Hills

I held her hand and walked
Among rumbling stones, among crackling
Rocks, through cracking caverns,
Up above splitting
Caves. Her curling, carved
Path was firm.

5. Sylvia's Forest

The trees were dreams. We wandered
All night by birches, by beeches,
Seeking the tree that should speak
The dawn. And fern
Rustled into oak, oak
Into wing. Then the phone.

What Then Is Love but Mourning

After the New Composition by Molpodora Melographos

I heard her song: song from song, lute
Lifting in April evening
Up the sides of skyscrapers, up
The blinking wings of planes, drifting down
Atmospheres, down the elevator shafts
Standing like hourglasses, down the hours
Of my breathing. She took her song
From a song; I took her song
For a walk. At the top of a tawny elm
A dove mourned, mourned, mourned.
And wings went singing above the suburbs of evening.

Molpodora's Gift

I touched the old song, and then the new.
The world altered, and I was almost changed.
It was now, and although my hand was still of then
And old breath filled my flute as old ink filled my pen,

I stumbled along her notes through Sinai, Saigon, Santiago,
Harlem, Concord, and felt in my sleepwalking step
What tunes I would play when I awoke at last
Out of the past.

Phegonaia

I.

The priestess of the beech
Is leaning on smoothness.

Ragged gifts lie limp in heaps.
In multitudes fecundities are swelling.

Under the young leaves the priestess is preaching
The year of the beechnut.

II.

What is the beechnut?
Something to count on,

Something to live on,
Forestall the squirrels for,

Roast over the hearth of your cave?
It is something she looked for.

Interpretation

The garden was not a garden
The oak was not an oak
Critics will tell you

And when I had closed the gate
Behind me I did not know
If I had entered

Or whether a laburnum dangling suns
In the universe of green and of the rain
Lived behind eyelids

Epistemology

Amid the mystical virgilias
We sniffed a sibylline perfume
As breezes blew us the prophecy:
Something.
Something is.

Is there something? As affirmations
Drift into July, there is always the question.

Beloved question! Amid the cataclysms
I hug you closer than being. Between your wings
I flap through the shaking air. Your fiery tongue
Is licking a lane through the smothering debris.
Is it?

Question

Is there a Greek garden?
June is cool
To my inquiry. Up in the wet elm
A blue jay is maintaining
That the cardinals have wrecked the weather.
On this old phonograph the nightingale squeaks.
In this small photograph the olive and the laurel
Blur and blend.
I see the stump of a chestnut,
The elegant skeleton of an elm.

Mythistorema

And what is Greece?
The Hellas of the Hellenes,
The other Rome of the Romans,
The goal of the glittering Americans
Four hundred thirty-four dirty dollars away?

They have planted an oak in my cold Dodona.
Karaghiozis is shaking his fist near the Athens Hilton.

And the oak is a beech,
And the laurel is a woman,
And the river is a father,
And Apollo smiles in the valleys,
And Zeus laughs on the mountains.

Prolegomena

You know that your Greece is real:
The kiosks, the buses, the goats,
The threshing and the dancing floors.

Or Greece is a quivering pillar
From the dragoned springs of earth
To the spread of the eagled sky.

I must quickly define my Greece
Before I am swallowed by the real
As the sea is swallowing the rocks.

June 21

How shall I map this land of the sun?
I stand between the expanse of aetherial fire
And these great solid undulations.
There the sea flames blue.

I have tramped far up to Dodona and under Olympus,
Marked the waves swinging around stout Sunium,
Sifted the Pylian sands,
Rested in Olympia's greenest grove.

I have watched a red sphere pause
On the gray western ridge.
I have seen the violet diadem of the city.
I have stood on this central rock and measured the mountains.

The mountains today have stepped forward in their ring, closer,
Or new lenses have been fitted to my eyes.

Before Vespers, August 6

His father is Darkness, his mother is Night.
I heard them clearly as we rumbled past.
That was their valley — and beyond,
Among the shrubs and rocks of Helicon, burst

Upon the August noon their cooling fountains.
I remember clutching a stick of bay
And noting that the vast clarity of the sky
Was muffled by no cloud and that no fleck

Of bitterness tinted the violet of their spring
And of their song because they knew the truth
In the stream that flows below the stony crust
Of mountains. I remember the tone.

His father is Darkness, his mother is Night,
His name is Aether.

Demeter

The pinkest rose, the bay, opens before
Her. Above, to the left, the flaming dragon tongues
Of black Eleusinian columns lick the pink air.

O red brilliance: A fire is rising
Into the sunsetting sky. Flinging back
Her black cloak she peers with red staring

Up the blue rocks above the bright buses
Rushing to toss behind them the highway,
The factories, the smokestacks, the smoke, the dust,

The dusk. In a place like this will I find my child?
Pale, purple-veined, the leafless autumn crocus
Rises among the brilliant falling leaves.

Muse

In somnolent summer he stood before me.

This is a Roman city. The high stone rostrum
Rings with long sonorities over the forum.
Small shops clatter. Visitors stroll
Through wide streets. Yet a trip to Corinth
Isn't for everyone. Streaming with green
And red, a pepper tree poses at the gate,
Luxuriant. Aged monolithic columns
Blink at the blue flash of the gulf.

I blinked as he stepped between the columns.
The hot rock under my feet echoed the white August glare.
He came close, shining like noon upon my bare head.
He smoothed back my hair. He moved
Light fingers over my lips.
I was touched. I was ready
For the day-bright rostrum.

I trembled as he stepped into the cella.
With nightfall, columns and walls had closed around a white fleece.
He came near, gleaming like marble among the clear stars.
He brushed back my hair. He moved
Firm fingers over my lips.
I was stirred. I was ready
For the night-dark mountain.

The bus is honking, the pepper tree flows
And flames, trumpets of radiance beam
From that cloud above the western peaks.
The bus is honking.

Biennial

I know the rhythms of my gardens
And the times of my flowers.
This is the shady narthex
To sunny hours

That will gush like fire from fennel
In a liturgy of fructification
Cascading through the nave from ray to runnel.

I, Promethean horticulturalist,
Flora the Prophet, foreknow
The month when the golden fruit will grow

In this ferny patch to unlock the gate
Into the central garden.
They cannot listen. "Now it is late,"

They roar with the winds of March. "And where
Are the buds, the silent pistils,
The stamens shaking gold through the air?"

It is excommunication. In a year I will laugh.
The apple key will blaze.
Who will claim those days?

I know the rhythms of my gardens
And the times of my fruit.
The first spring gleams in my arbor.
They want me out.

Theater

I sat on the hillside. Did a royal car
Cross the circle to deliver from afar
Two whose proud and wavering tread
On crimson made me face the dead?

I saw gigantic Hymettus prone.
I saw some tourists trying a throne.
I heard the traffic of Sunday afternoon
And, from a cypress, the cicadas' dry tune.

Theogamy

For a moment I had to close my eyes.
Why was I in tears
When I faced the ochre columns of Apollo
Glowing below the gleam of the Delphic cliffs
That shielded the goal of my twining road
Like the walls of a radiant cave?

Once in a dusky cave,
Not far from my father's house on the crest
Of the rock ruling Athens,
I put down my flowers on the stone
And sensed the golden breath
And loved the young god.

Diary of Flora Baum
Delphi, Bysios 7

The priestess is gone, and the poet.
The roof is gone, and the fire.
Six drab columns band
The shining vertical vast crags.

Infant laurels guard the ramp
To the empty temple. What shall I do?
Down among glittering olives Athena stands
As calm as when she stepped from the mind of the sky.

The sky is the roof.
The sky holds the fire.
The earth holds the sky. I rest
In the friendly groove of a headless post.

Does he wander in Tempe,
Winter in England,
Turn back to Lycia, to light, to the wolf,
Love a tree?

Down among the olives a serpent twines
About the tree at Athena's side.
Water sprinkles the cliffs.
Earth rattles the columns.

Oracles

You saw the eagles at Delphi, climbed by night
Up Parnassus, up to the place of contest;
I sat at the foot of the cliff, at the foot of a column,
And heard the swallows twitter in the August sunset;
I ventured at noon from the shade of a little laurel
And stepped straight into the hell of the sun-topped temple
And begged the god: "What great thing shall I do?"

"Be your own prophet." The answer shimmered in glare.

The Garden of Hephaestus

The flower pots are in the museum. The flowers
Are here. The lithe, the live shrubs are a song
To the lyre of the columns of the temple on the hill. In the light
Of north and south and west, on gleaming green,

Twinkle little myrtle stars, tinkle
Carmine pomegranate bells. And to the east
The porch of the god stares out upon the dust
And skeletons of the ancient city's glory.

Beyond magenta oleanders, beyond
Laurels, silvered olives, golden pines,
The long brown mountains soften into violet.
The sun sets on the cicadas and the subway.

Guards have barred the gates to the darkened garden.
Hephaestus is hammering flowers of fire in the sky.

Mneme

There was something I wanted to say
When I reached the rocky top of my desire
And blinked upon beauty.

The central orchestra of stone,
Smooth, grooved, and true,
Lay yet solid under my sandals.

Suddenly I moved
Among the companies of statues rising
Strong and tall from a titanic sowing
In the gleam of marble and bronze.

Suddenly I passed
The rapid walls and the rushing roof of Athena's house.
I held the hands of the dancing Attic ghosts
And stepped the reverent rites of this theater,

Knowing that from the great circle of their seats —
Blue benches of Salamis, Aegaleos, and Parnes,
Bright marble boxes of Pentelicus,
Thrones on bold Hymettus and faint Aegina —

Divinities were watching till the circle closed,
Gazing till the scene became the sea.
The Attic ghosts all sank.

There was something I wanted to say
As I stumbled through the rubble, among the shambles,
In the clasp of grand fragments.

Part Four

Odyssey

Proto-Pasch

Those slips of lavender,
Sudden, pale, rain-radiant, on that spot
Beyond the ashes of the snow,
Spoke to us as we stood
In February: We move
In a movement that is large. They stood
Small and rain-straight, over there,
In the vestments of a Lent of light,
And jays were bells in the reddish campaniles
Of maples, and the whole church of the world
Lurched toward March.

Part Five

The Diagram

Dactylography

My fingers on these keys
Cannot make music. This instrument
Is never tuned, is never played,
Is operated. This is work.
The operator is another
Instrument, with fingers wired
Straight to the executive's brain.
He thinks, dictates, executes.
Thus she spoke from the rack of the day.
The racket under her hands went on.

Even without strawmen,
Even without snowmen,
January is a bad time to begin.
Everything is hard and cold and small.
The muscles of the megalopolis
Jerk into stillness. Contraction
Claws crowds standing by the silent tracks.
Where is that expansive tree? The crows
Gnash their beaks at the year.
The cold rhododendron paws have stiffened.
She keeps a stiff upper lip.
There's something she's trying to find.

Somewhere over the rainbow,
Once in a blue moon,
Down there among the daisies,
Every morning in June,
Slight, spare, under the snowflakes,
Rich, rare, under the flashlight,
Flitters a tune.

Ice.
A glass river,
An iron river,
A river of steel.
Only wind moves,
Wind slipping over ice.

Steel.
A room of steel,
A little room,
A little chair jammed next to glass.
A wind of steel,
Wind shot through one breach.

If the wind would blow to the end of March.
Light lasts. Color kindles.
Embers of elm blossom, tawny at noon,
Glow in the sunset like robin song,
With robin song. Enlargement begins.

She was born to grandeur in a vertical world.
Millions of windows glitter
Fired from ocean or continent.
The tiny, spikey island's gigantic
Spikes are orange flames.
Sunrise dreams from the sea,
But not through eastern windows only
Laps light at the edge of eveningland.

She was born to grand landscapes of horizon.
From beside the sky-shoulderer's sea
Long slim fingers of shadow
Point toward the sea called peaceable.
And back across Nevada, across Nebraska, across Indiana
Stretch the deictic fingers of the sun
Painting the Empire State's sharp nail.

Aged nine and six, ribboned and flounced,
Up the elevator she and Flossie led
Grandma to show her "our view."
They had never been before, but the place was theirs —
Their vantage point, their landmark, the center, cosmic omphalos.

When at seven she tried her first glasses
Fine lines high on that spire
First gratified her gaze.
This was vision, this acuity.
This you look to for anchor,
This you look from to measure the world.
This is lovely, this is beautiful,
This is the growth of your soil.

Do you love a building
Like a tree, like a mountain,
Like a bright soaring melodious bird?

The big bird sat on her big nest.
An eagle was it, or a cuckoo?
Megalopolis americana americana
It seemed to the nestling.

The tail feathers sparkle with capital
Illuminations. The mandibles
Devour the print of ages in Widener
Library. You can't confine her.
Watch her wings unfurl, a tip
Touch Attu, a tip tap Athens.
The ever-hatching egg: Manhattan.
The modus operandi: Zip.

From such a nest
Fledgling Flora set forth on her quest.

Where do you go from here?
She fell upon the stage of clerk-typist,

Drumming out the drear
Business of others, which the tight fist

Of however determined self
Can't even grasp as pelf.

How could she fall
Into ways where you have to crawl,

She, the biped, the walker,
Her footprints in the hardened African ash,

She of the tree-climbing hands,
The free, the plume-clasping hands,

She of the flying pen,
Of the wingèd words,

She, the talker,
Forced to gnash

Her beak as the conversing men
Think her thoughts are for the birds

And she is part of the furniture,
Set up in the corner,

A coat rack, a coffee burner,
Stamp stamping another's signature?

How could she fall
Into realms where the mind's a thrall?

When she was out looking
Why didn't she look out?

Again, what was she looking for?
Ah, the finer lines,

The melody of light,
The great opening door

Into the shimmering hall
Beyond the signs?

Somewhere over the rainbow
Where there's a booking

THE DIAGRAM

Beyond all doubt
After the main show?

With the chirping and whistling of ice
On the pond, the witchhazel fingers
Reach out. Then they retract.
After the long retrenchment we reach out again
As frolic bubbles up through mud
And trickles through the brownish frills of the elm,
She thought. She thought:
We live in drops, in ticks, in fingertaps.
Her digital hands clap on —
Praiseless clappers in a tuneless bell.
Mais la lumière . . .

                In wavering April
Beyond the lying lifeless leaves
The leafless azaleas come on.
Their pure allure
Allumes a region.
A lavender disposition of light
Is wrought behind the small wrought-iron fence.
Behind the black elegance of point and curve and bar
Plays the fixed instant of the dance of lavender wings.
Other suspensions: nestling-green,
Rose-centered barberry drops.
Other centers: orange shouts
In the purple hymns of crocus.
Deep-pool-blue squills are to lawns
As stars to Delphic skies.
Other shining outbursts: tufted
Titmouse, crested cardinal,

Prophesying, preaching, wooing.
Behind the battered stockade
Forsythia kisses the breeze with golden abandon.
Breezes wheel. Winds reverse.
Gray gulls gleam and gloam.
There's a January shiver.

A genuine snowperson, she.
She keeps a stiff upper lip.
Her back, her face, her brain
Are rigid. Her hands prance on
At a breadwinning clip.

The main show's the dinner,
Then there's the song?

In a little wood in Washington,
Right in the capital city, sang a bird
Through the leaves of evening.

Over here. Come and play.
Never fear. Don't delay.
Come away. Over. Never astray.
Over here. Hear my claim.
Here no one grieves.
Know my face, know my name.
Here no one deceives.
But all the woods grew dim.
The shadows of leaves.

When Pocahontas heard the nightingale
She sighed for the woodthrush.

In a little desert near Los Angeles,
Right near the far-flung city, bloomed a flower
Through the spread of noon.

This is no mirage.
This fragrant gift is a first of May
In my own dimidium of earth.

This unearthly earth is the land of the cacti —
Globes and poles, hassocks and snakes,
Shapes of my hemisphere, vegetable monsters,
Most unreal, with most real floraison.

Here is a breathing barrel topped by a yellow blossom.
Here is that living prickly cylinder
Petaled with softest of harmonies (lavender
Blended of pinks and whites): the echinopsis.

A twittering dove hovers above the yucca,
The mockingbird thrills over tufted agaves,
While a busy fellow-citizen, the whizzing little lizard,
Traffics in the shadow of the giant saguaro.

The deepest blue-green bloom of the puya
Chalices a sparkle of orange
Not far from the planted camels of the west:
Rooted hedgehogs, pincushions, naily throttles.

This is no mirage.
These spiny, bloated monsters hold forth beauty
And survive.

She flew over her land. Monster and flower.
She flew over her land. Beauty and beast.

In the merry month of May,
In terra aliena, in the other half of the world,
She found the things that she knew:

Gray castles by gray seas,
White posts under blue skies,
Mighty circles that could stop a Xerxes
With his thousands —
The great plane tree,
The old holm oak —,
The yew that Pontius Pilate saw,
The olive tree that Plato loved,
The fresh bright larch,
The dark cedar,
Traffic by Hadrian's Arch,
Bracken by Hadrian's Wall,
Cuckoo, curlew,
Lapwing, lark,
Swallow, swift, and swan.

She played sun to the revolving lapwing,
Earth to his epicycles,
Intelligence to the squeaking of his spheres.
The earth was gliding beneath the curlew's wild wail,
While above the braided hills
Rose the measured frenzy of an ever-diminishing dot,
An unstopping period. Then it stopped,
It dropped,
As the resonating cuckoo went on telling a long time,
And across the lake came the wing song,
The swan song.

Here, where the nightingale
Did not sing, was silence.

In the perfect days of June
Virgilias extended magic wands
Or yellowwoods extended golden boughs.

Here you are in the fourth direction.
A whitening grove
Lazes along the top of Appleton Street,
Sanctifies the top of Appleton Street.
The frangible branches are hung with pearls.
The wands are trimmed with white fillets.
The gold is white gold.
The gold gold lies beneath.
Panicles, rank upon rank,
Form and flourish. Arthur and his host
Might lie beneath, rise, ride forth
With the bugle before.
Fragrance, wave upon wave,
Slips up the shore
With the undulations of mourning doves,
The spray of their wings bidding: Pilgrimage, pilgrimage,
And from their throats
Flowing an ocean's decree: Honor heroes now.

Where Professor Longfellow walked
His grounds toward the curving Charles,
Virgilias flower. Near where Professor Holmes
Took breakfast, a yellowwood smiles
On budding economists and econometrists.
Outside Professor Lowell's window
A courtly virgilia stands in fine lace observing
The elegant eighteenth-century clapboard house
From which Harvard's president cycles daily to work.
In the old botanic garden
Beside the spot where Professor Gray
Labeled his flora, papilionaceous bloom
Sweetens the breeze in the parking lot. Was it here,
Where the long white clusters preside
Over purple commencement in Harvard Yard,
That Professor Child wooed the virgilia, took
The tender tips of its fingers in his hands?

The sibylline fingers hold blossoms,
Each marked with a blotch of gold.

In the center sirens sing.
Fuming, Boreas, Eurus, Zephyrus, Notus
Hurtle through hard corridors.

Americans can't adapt.
Look at all those foreigners:
Pigeons, starlings, sparrows,
Pallid ginkgoes, tough ailanthuses.
How the rock dove loves these cliffs!
How the tree of heaven fits
Into these cracks!

A native, can't she adjust to a piece of rock?
How her hometown touches heaven!

In the micropolis. South:
The music on the executive's
Radio went too far.
She could not hear it. West:
The daffodils died in the jar.
They could not make it. East:
From nine to five the cuckoo called non-stop.
North: Her fillet had begun to knot.
Center: The pit of her stomach held a rock.

Over his keys the musing organist
First lets his fingers wander as they list.
Over her keys
She cannot make music,
She cannot muse.
Tell me, muse.
No tune, no play, pure operation,
Smooth, selectric, self-correcting.
What self corrected, selectrified?
With the self the pain is lifted away
By the key that cannot move forward.
So turn it back.

Tell me, muse, the man of many turns,
The wandering,
Tell me the woman of many strands,
Wound and unwound,
The epic of Penelope.
By day one weaves the web of words,
By night the correcting key
Clicks back, back, back, over the lines,
Lifting every letter from every page
As every thought was lifted from the muzzled brain.
Here and here are the lines of the binding web,
There and there the blanks where the key
Touched and took.
The traveller or the unraveller — which is stranded?

Seizure rhymes with leisure.
Carpe diem.
Pleasure rhymes with leisure.
Epi nea.

Our days are short.
Ice holds our long shore.

The American elm is a winter tree,
Fine in nakedness, like a young Greek at play.
It rises above its native cold. It does not stiffen.
Its form soars from the hardened earth
And easily returns bestowing ease.

But January shrank this great old elm,
Americana through and through.
It must have been the greatness
That could not take the cold,
The denudation. One saw sticks,

Not as in April, when its fingers
Fling light scarves of coppery lace
About its shoulders, adornment
For the body's vernal exercise,
Not as in June, when it stretches into summer.

The cat's paws scratched down the trunk,
Thudded onto the soil,
Whisked cat noiseless through the hedge.
High in the branches the little birds were whimpering.

Sing of the flickering rose at the top of the oak in the laughter
Trilling the rhythms of gleam and of breeze through the musk of the
    morning.
Butterflies flit through the columns. The polaroid click of my eyelids
Catches the flitting, the fluting, the white rest, rosier gold-winged
Breath, high reach of the oak toward the high rhododactylous dawning.
Sing the return of the day, sleepy muse; it is long after sunset.

By day I work the shuttle
On a worthless web.
By night I am Ulysses
Confronting the stars.

Sing the evening gest.
Sing the weekend hero.
Just wait till we get our two weeks of vacation.

The executive is waiting.
These fingers are not mine.
The executive is speaking
To his fingers,
To a hand,
To the cat's paw.

The great old elm in August
Was not exhausted.
The leaves were fresh as raindrops.
The trunk was young as thunder.
The branches stormed into the sky.
The wind kept laughing in the leaves.
What was that golden wing scratching the path?

The oak that August
Was not the biggest
And not the oldest,
Yet a shining pyramid rose from the lawn.
Over the lawn
Around the gray pillar
A distance grew.
A butter-gold butterfly occupied the distance.
The lawn went on. The tree
Reached up and touched a bird
Flying from the sky. The sky,
Coming into the orbit of the oak, drew it higher.

Who makes music when the birds grow silent?
What incessant melodist steps onto the stage?
A song of August ascended from the oak.
She saw green sun, she saw white sun,
She saw at the vertex a glitter of stars.

The pin oak is a winter tree.
It stands stiff and gray against the January light.
The song of the wolf — is that a January song?

Her boss was an editor named Eliot.
He asked: Why have you hung your dirty linen?
The typist home. The electric fire.
She asked: What have you done to April?

Her boss was a professor named Pound.
He said: You have not modernized yourself.
The cage was closing. No. To the ship.
She said: My Chinese is poor.

Her boss was a lawyer named Stevens.
He asked nothing. He said nothing.
Every page she typed he tossed to the floor.
She crawled in dirty silence.

O my fathers. I wasn't born in armor.

That day she had to keep wielding
The steel unstapling claws.

The blue squills by the path under the flashlight
On her way to the steps
Gleamed as the blue lights gleam along the runway
Before there is nothing but hum and stiff black wing
Far beyond cloud.

When she moved up the river
A little way out of the city
She thought she'd see big mother osprey
Settle on the telephone-pole platform by the third-story window
As she would on a pinetop near a blue lake,
Calmly looking straight into the wind
And gently turning her warm eggs
While her great nest and the platform and the pole
Grew orange, grew aureate in the sunset.
Herr House Sparrow took the stage,
Performing to his perched
Admiring fräulein audience.

What shall I say about the late subscribers?
Seven times each name and address
Emerges from my fingers:
Once onto the sharp blue file card
(These same fingers, even if wounded,
Will put that in its place),
Once onto the white Cheshire label card
(Information to be reproduced
Must be within broken blue lines),
Once onto the short form letter
(It is our pleasure to inform you),
Once onto the long white envelope
(Fed to the choking Pitney-Bowes
Date-spitting, flap-licking, touchmatic postage meter),
Three times onto the thin gummed labels
(Stuck to the wrappers of back issues
Stuffed in the narrow back room).

One time you'll start those labels
And you won't stop.
You'll extend your thumb and index finger,
Daintily extract a thin sheet,
Suspend it backwards and upside down,
Nudge the throttle to make it chug in,
Hustle your fingers into their places.
Here's the "j" and here's the "a."
                                                        Oh,

Oh, Ms. Bonnie Hellyon Bray,
2468 Wither Way,
Apartment number 13K,
Stopoff comma space PA,
Or perchance it is MA,
02468. ESSAIS,

Apr 79. Away . . .
Extend your thumb, extract the prey.
You do the millionth sheet today.
Oh, Ms. Bonnie Hellyon Bray,
This is but play.

My fingers
Cannot make music.
A hum under my fingers —
Its hum.
A rhythm against my fingertips,
Altering my fingerprints —
Its rhythm.
Vibration entering my fingers,
Entering into my blood,
Pulsing up to my heart —
Its vibration.
Its fingers,
Its blood,
Cannot make music.

Sp,ewjere pver tje raombpw.
Pmce om a b;ie ,ppm.
Dpwm tjere a,pmg tje daosoes.
Everu ,prmomg om Kime.
S;ogjt. s½are. imder tje smpwf;ales.
Rocj. rare. imder tje f;asj;ogjt.
F;otters a time/

Time —
How it f;otters.
It limps through the day.
These hands fly on a machine
Smooth as a 747.
Yon clock's hands crawl:
9:28, 9:44, 9:59, 10:13, 10:26.
We'll go the way the elephant goes,
We'll never get there,
Wringing our hands.

Her hands kept hammering away.

She put up a sign for father osprey:
Danger! All fish on this continent
Likely to be contaminated for some time.
Try us again in about a decade.
Trucks kept passing. She couldn't hear
The sound of her hammer. She couldn't smell
The lilacs by the gate. There were lilacs.

The traffic passed Hadrian's Arch through

The Athens of the Athenians,
The Athens of the Romans,
The Athens of the Americans,

The Athens of the drachma,
The Athens of the denarius,
The Athens of the dollar,

The Athens of the golden oil.

Do children work in America?
Asked the *mikrós* in the Delphic restaurant.

Here you're never more than a girl.
You can't be a woman.
You certainly can't be a man.
You undoubtedly couldn't feel human.
Why, you're a couple of hands,
A dizaine of digits. What wonder
If you're all thumbs?

Do you wonder?

The small white flowers grow wild
By the common woodland paths.
Then why must she climb like the bear
Above the rough waterfall, sliding her feet,
Grasping the jagged rocks with her fingers,
To peer at the small white flower
Dancing its sword dance in the violence of the wind?

Do you wonder? Do you think?

Do you think the executive has a headache?
Do you think the executive has an ulcer?
Was Bill expelled last March from his prep school?
Was Susie drowned last June in the swimming pool?
Does it seem that Mrs. Straw will recover
Now that the mastectomy is over?
Has the doctor warned him to cut down on steak?
Shall I smile now for the executive's sake?

The stiff white Cheshire label card
Grins as you squint at the pale
Broken blue lines, press tab, clear tab,
Set tab, press tab. Tabby,
Reproduce that information,
This will need no confirmation,
This is only decoration,
One, two, three, a nation.

This will keep the nation going,
Keep the flow of paper flowing.
Take the key and lock her up,
Lock her up, lock her up.
Dam the spluttering cascade,
One, two, three, a maid.

Nine, ten, a locked-up pen,
Eleven, twelve, dig and delve,
Seventeen, eighteen, maid awaiting —
Waiting on five.
When will it arrive —
Time to be alive?
Will she survive?

Summoned by the beech-green light
She crossed the rain-green lawn
In the sun of an unending afternoon,
Gentle successor to insistent rain.
And, when the bellowing hawk had cleared
The blue and droned to port
(Concorde bent on Heathrow
Over Kew in lilac time),
She stood among white trees of cloud,
Green trees of tree,
And could not move.
The thrush-throbbed melismata of blackbirds,
The throbbing glisten of the grove
Of beech and bluebell, the throbbing fragrance
Of ocher rhododendron held her: lump
Fixed in magnetic streams. And, casually
Munching, from Tibet, arrayed
In purple cape and zebra train
And scarlet robe and golden crown,
A golden pheasant sauntered in.
What syllable was sung
Between the bluebells and the blue?
If one image could subsume
The golden bird and the golden bloom,

The

The golden scent and the golden tune,
The golden, golden afternoon . . .

Night. Why do our fingers
Fumble and fail? Why do our hands
Grope and clench and sag?
Night. New York. Why do I touch
Gray stone, gray cloud? Why do I feel
Sharp claw, sharp beak? Sharp feathers slip
From my pillow, drift to the floor.
Barefoot I ford the room.
Lights churn on the ceiling.
How did I lose my touch?
How did I lose the key?
My sharp screeching, my flat moaning
Ask the sirens. The sirens answer:

Beauty is sometimes sharp,
Beauty is sometimes gray,
Sometimes a bluet, sometimes an elm
Expanding into the sky.

Speed up the machine,
Make it do the work,
Slow down hours of dream and play,
Sometimes stop the clock.

Try to quench the fumes,
Try to brake the noise,
Try to stretch your arms and find
The soft bright melodic breeze.

We'll go the way the airplane goes.
We'll surely get there.

In Stuyvesant Park the fountain
Played. She saw a pigeon
Scarved in beginnings of rainbow.

A big bird. A small park.
A small park. A big city.
A big city. A little beauty.

Flying from Maine to Miami,
Less than an hour out of Boston look to the right.
If you see a small island,
See its splendors rising,
Light, airy, vertical,
Rising cleanly, effortlessly, in silence,
See an enchanted plot
Lifting its shining oak trees,
See arms raised in the great
Climax of a great ballet,
Won't you sing?

Somewhere cities gleam,
Somewhere bluets bloom,
Somewhere lightning plays on the peaks,
Crimson flowerets hide on the oaks,
Fingers find their notes,
Tunes are bright fruits.

The Fire Escape

1. Sky

It is propitious
When the clusters of samaras match the bricks
And gusts in the dry clusters
Match the flaps of the pigeons
And a white slant across the black slats
Mirrors the darks of the dapples of backs
And the straight metalled edge of the tall red horizon adjacent
Meets blue deepening.

Can I cut a temple in the sky
And see the eagles pass auspiciously?

Blue, cloudless, that was the first way she remembered it.
It was the first thing she remembered.
You could rest in it wherever you moved —
Manhattan, Brooklyn, Chicago, Delphi.
Was it the same in Delphi?

When the epigones piled up the columns again
A particular verticality reappeared —
That of man, the erect, the geometer,
The astronaut. Far above the cliffs
Eagles sailed among the stars.

In the city, locus of the marks of man —
The straight border, the measured line,
The parallel, the perpendicular, the plumb —
In the city, sky was indicated.
There might not be much of it, but you looked up,
Pretending not to so you wouldn't be noticed —
Above all you wanted not to be noticed —
You pretended to look down so you wouldn't be noticed —
But you looked up. At the end
Of the measured lines lay the sky.

There was that blue one over the red brick building,
On top of the even, counted rectangles.
That one you could sit and watch.
The old red blanket had been spread out on the slats.

Here, remember, there was no earth.
There was no air.
Below, at times, illegally released
From fire hydrants, water ran red.
The aether was the elemental thing,
Blue fire.

Intensest melody,
Voice from the doorway of being,
Hyacinth of existence,
Essence of forget-me-not,
Penetrant into the self's
Cerulean penetralia,
Throbbing with the sapphire
Throbbing of reflective self
Straight out to the edges of quest and question,

O be forever blue, unending patch.
But by then the steady flash was broken,
The azure species flattened.
It was not clouds, night, a closing of lids;
That fleeing of the gleam from behind wide-open eyes,
That was it. The morning-glory curls.
The squill in the brick-red pot has faded.
The bars grow cold against the bones of your back.

2. Tree

She saw the single, multitudinous elm.

The trunk with its primary branches
Is firm, is still. A motion inheres
In that stillness: all the growing, the upholding,
The struggle recorded in a stance —
Antaeus kept from the earth,
The discus almost hurled,
A slain god just arisen.

The moving branchlets with their moving
Leaves are at rest, are not uneasy,
Are at ease, are resting as unresisting,
As swans rest on the stirring stream,
As eagles rest on the warm drafts of late morning.

Here is a solitary being, self-contained
And self-directed; here two hug and kiss;
Here is the generous outreach, proffering
Of gifts; then follow revel, bacchanal
Of lifted arms, green brands alight,
Frisson of verdure; ladies come
With fans and trailing gowns.

A form, a formulation, an assertion
Builds as clauses rise and phrases dangle
Into a green flutter of interjections
Among which cluster golden promises,
Promising the post-autumnal blank.

Buds supply the wintry punctuation.

3. Season

Of significant instants in the shifting of the sun
That of September is felt the least.
One point in December holds a community's jubilation:
From now the days will be getting longer.
One March moment is a general celebration:
Now the days are getting longer.
June's peak is a public joy:
Now we see the longest day.
People petal streets and parks and beaches.
Eternal splendor gilds the common sun.
September twenty-third slipped by
With a cool exhalation across a red leaf.
She put on her plaid skirt. At supper
The windows were down,
The shades were down,
The lamp was on,
The book was open.
Life was private.

4. Temple

September becomes a place,
September becomes a temple,
And an hour of September is a cella in that temple,
A cell in which the monk walks up and down.
Walking is a moving of the eyes
In one place in one vision. Tears
Are not forming. Pears
Hang as dropped from their blossoms.
Full, the fern-leaf beech, with sky at its brim,
Uplifts, keeps on uplifting.
Uplifted, fresh as of spring, slender and green,
The pagoda tree's fruits and leaves, with sky between,
Rest in ecstatic levitation.
All is green and glitter, all is light and light,
Beneath the benevolent blue.

THE DIAGRAM

You find no long liturgy here,
No choirs, no stanzaed songs,
But brief petitions, terse monitions,
Eleison exclaimed, short sounds
Of blue- or red-vested priests on their rounds.

Then a quiet.

What is that behind me?
Who is that walking behind me?
Those are the first footsteps
Of the first fallen leaves.

Would these panes always stand
Between her and the world?
She wept. She was only seven.
The high fine lines were apocalyptic.
The tallest building in the world
Had darkly stood before her eyes.
She could bear to see through glass.

In the large room of November —
A hall for a Hrothgar —
The posts and beams were bared,
Some flames still flickered in the barberry hearths,
The golds and greens and coppers gleamed
In the tapestry of the beech.
Of the dancing, nothing remained
But the gray whack of her heels on the sidewalk,
The brown crackling under her soles,
The skirl and drone of leafblowers puffing over lawns.
The huge room of November
Was a home for a Massachuset
Silently crossing his brown carpet.

Along the street
Last fire,
Last gold —
Barberry fire,
Beech gold —
Flicker and glint
As dark slants on.

Closing,
She knows
A flicker,
A glint
In that dark.
There's a fire in there
Growing leaves of gold.

Night is very long.
I have slept even in the day.
I have slept even through the spring.
Even in November
New flowers are fresh.
The blooming witchhazel freshens
Above its failing leaves.
The rose is as fresh and white as the threatening snow.

She feels the flower of fire
In the sunset of late autumn
Before the astrology begins,

Before the Saracen princess Fleurdefeu
Can utter her predictions of victory and defeat.
The fire and the flower are victory.

If light ensues, if fruits
Lie piled in the cellars, if cold
Skips on the borders, a document

May enter the tradition. If a feeling
Bloomed, a vision burned, an autumn
Echoed for a moment, she fared well.

Oh, cut it out, shouts the jay.
Ah, remember that friend
Of Mother and Dad's who knew Sandscript?
Oh, remember how the el
At a certain spot used to bite its tail
Almost? Ah, remember tonsils
And the taste of wood? Oh, remember
Writing in the moist and salty sand?

Now she'll cut out
A contemporary temple
In compartments. Segments,
Sections, cuttings, clippings
Constitute her bricks; for instance,
The universe is smaller than we thought.
We thought there was a hotter fire.
We thought of a gleam beyond the massed atoms of the stars.

Post no bills,
It said on the gray sky.

Now she'll settle for a temple of bricks,
But then a temple of marble,
Then the showy echo of Pentelicus
Will rise around her as she climbs the steps
Up to the desired sidereal sheen.
Now it is possible to consider
To what music it will then be possible to hearken,
For what kudos it will then be possible to scavenge.
Caveat desiderator. Yet
The temple is loved for itself.
She surely can't help it if its acoustics
Are those of the mountains and the constellations.

So many oh's have turned into ah's.
There's one in the deodar, timber of the gods
Of Kamet and Kangra and Kew,
Of Karakoram and California.

The desideratrix
Can consider
The bricks.

It's easier to see
On a cloudy day
Looking out of

A dirty window
When it's too cold
To sit outside.

Some are redder,
And some are browner.
The day is browner.

Up to a certain height
The brown veins cling
Though the red drops are gone.

Their new storm windows
Are richly edged with brown.
They'll keep warm.

Her radiator is sputtering,
The grayed frames around her panes sag,
As she sits in her brown study.

Watch out,
You're staring south-east,
And it's morning.

What was the world,
What was herself,
And what was God
She now sits with closed eyes
And sees. The sparrows scrape their violins,
The radiator pipes up through its piccolo,
The drumsticks of the clock tap on, mutually tapping.
What was the green world,
What was her purple self,
What was the blueness of divinity
She now discovers achromatic
Against the orange of her eyelids.
The soprano of the refrigerator rises.
Scales fall from the ceiling.
I see men like trees but walking about.
Since these enchanting lineaments
Wait for her scrutiny, she looks.
The trees are a tree. The men are a man.
The slow kaleidoscope
Accepts her focus. The tree fills the screen.
It is not a tree. It is a dance.
Its beat beats in her chest,
Incarnates itself throughout her flesh.
Immovable, she feels it move.
When the dancer lays hands upon her eyes
She sees the subject of the motionless rhythm.
In the beginning, before there was movement, this dance was packaged,
And since this idol, unwrapped, exists, she surrenders.
She hears its speaking in her ears
Above the fluting of the police car,
Below the saxophoning of the truck,
Beyond the tenor of the airplane like an angel in the sky.

If the vehicle were the tenor
She would understand those who said:
Too many trees. Too florid. Too much chrome.
The trees composed an alphabet. The words
Loomed larger, like forests. The sentences . . .
Meaning shimmered through the vast
Aposiopesis. On the gold-fringed oak
She sought the fresh red drop that antedated the acorn.
The vehicle was the tenor.
The tree was trusty and true.
The dryad was its coeval.
She was the druid who saw the oak.
It was that pin oak, Quercus palustris,
Seen in that place, seen on that day and that.

It was not a good time
For seeing the oak —
The anniversary of the murder.
He had dragged her into the park.
He left her stripped and shot.
Thanksgiving weekend, people said,
Everyone out of town.
The potentate went on to live his life.
But the traffic must have kept passing
At four-thirty on a Saturday afternoon.
One is always shutting out the traffic.

November is not the time
For this oak. The oak has speckled the grass
With its brown scraps. It sticks up colorless,
Cracked, and knobby into a spotty sky.
A blue jay lays harsh, confident claim
To its heights. The gray gains timbre,
Inevitably gets to ascend in the center
Of the green lawn. It gets to be a monody
With ramifications, with sky-domed fine
Filamental resonances.

They

They do almost fly off in the end,
But the mass is material, rooted, trim.
Behind, the colorful traffic gives
A diffident accompaniment. From the strewn green plane
Through the solid tight-bound trunk
To the explicit linearities of the tips
An integral, an ultimate . . . Who is this capped character
That has seated himself, twiddling his thumbs,
Between me and my contemplation?

Poor Flora. What does she need?
A little clapboard shuttered house
In the suburbs, a little back yard,
A flowery patch, a tree or two
Within the fence? Purdah,
Claustration? Does Little Red Riding Hood need
A chaperon, a chape, a coat of mail?

A remembered temple in a remembered sky.
A remembered temple in an actual sky.
An actual temple in a remembered sky.
These are possible. But it's too cold
For too much actuality. Either your windows
Are streaked or your eyes water. And it's too bright,
Too early on the eve of Advent for a hymn
To the dews of heavens past. The sparrows
Have just relinquished their harping. Then set
The actual in the remembered. Ignore
Your bricks splashed on the opposite windows.

The old red blanket had been spread out on the slats.
Maybe it wasn't old then. Once it must have been new.
The sky was new. It surpassed Manhattan.
It stretched beyond ken and kenning,
Earth-holder, eye-opener, edge-toucher, mind-rouser.
Tall buildings whirl. Straight lines waver. Parallels crash.
It stays there, smoothly deepening. Build while it's still,
Still ô ciel azur, ó céu azul.

A blue background. That will do for a while.
Branching in a December dusk,
On late azure, on early rose.
That will do. A sudden shift
To greenest Florida or greenest June
With brightest flittings. That will serve.
We suppose — superpose — the same sky,
Turning the lights up or down,
Filling or clearing the stage.

Branches are cut in the watchet
Letting the black show through
And the black is punctured with gleams
Like Manhattan from the Esplanade at night
And the stars come rushing to the boughs
Not like sparrows, not like eagles,
Like suns volleying to earth.

We thought our dominoes were cities,
And they fell as bowling pins fall.

A quieter version. A sky of prussian blue.
The black December branches cold and clear.
Or something like this. Design without design.
A urobore. A Celtic decoration.
Decus. Something like this. Here it is.

O fortunate whose cities rise!
In a grove in the center at the crest of the hill
You begin to see against the sky,
As she points, the bronzen portals hoisted,
The marble metopes carved and hued.

The child sat in relief with her knees drawn up,
Her little marble fingers clasped around them.
She seemed to rest against niello stripes.
Her eyes of lapis lazuli looked out,
Her face tilted up. And whence is this to me?
VISITATIO was the inscription.

The next read DURA. A marble oak
Would never shed its emerald leaves
In mere November. Slender nymphs
Dancing in green around the tree
Were tougher than duramen, strong
As stone, unchipped, unbrokenhearted.

Tyrian birds in a Mycenaean sky,
Three purple birds that sing in a sky of gold,
Like a trio of strings that sound in a golden hall,
Shimmer and glide over CONTEMPLATIO, cutting across wide
Space, through long time, and no wings rise or fall
And no bows swiftly shift or slowly hold
Before the blinking of the augur's eye.

Above CAUTA, like a cardinal that clicks
Through the chill into the December sun,
A slim woman in a ruby dress
Of velvet was bent over cuneiform,
Impressing what she had observed, for the fire
Reddened well within the frame.

On the blank but candid panel gleamed a star,
And then a twin appeared, and soon a third,
And then a fourth, and soon a constellation
Was sprayed like orange sunrise. Then the wise,
Amazed, were gazing, saying: Where is he?
Carved letters spelled DESIDERATIO.

5. Season

Boots are pulled on.
The sun stops.
It is called winter.

Snow is refashioning New England.
Snow has halted New York.
Snow has glittered all day across the Plains and over the Rockies.
Along the Pacific there's nothing but precipitation.

Here the bugs sang all last night.
Only the writhing cajeputs are white.
Under the ramrod palms you stroll in sandals through the evening light.

6. Tree

The etymology, the genuine speech,
Here stutters. But the Malay derivation
Is given: cajeput, white tree.
The Austronesian roots don't speak to me.
These trees seem rootless, seem to stand
On the close-clipped grass as in an opaque
Green mere. You'd think their feet were
Planted on a shallow, unseen bottom.
And still they're flourishing, though far from home.
Florida, said Flora, is the land of flowers.

From the screened porch, with its seasonable
Show of red and green — blooming
Christmas cactus, poinsettias with subtended
Inflorescence, tannenbaum with its suspended
Efflorescence, among the watering cans —
Beyond a square of screen, beyond the glare
Of the parking lot, across the glint of the road,
In the ample stripe of green beside
The path along the gold wall in front of the gold
Buildings, silver-balconied, bronze-tile-roofed

(Discreetly

(Discreetly gold the buildings, the long wall, refined,
Although the sky is indiscreetly blue,
Blazingly, unblushingly, insistently noon-blue
In cloudless noon over stiff gold buildings), you see
The cajeputs with fuzzy tops,
With feathery, green-gray-haired heads
Lost in whitish cloudlets, with white thighs
Discreetly white. We walked along the path
Beside the line of cajeputs, along the path, along . . .

The trunks are finger-painted in high relief;
The foliage is brush-painted, with the vagueness
Of the brush; the flowers, from the porch, no longer
Brushes, no longer clouds, are stars. We had seen
And were come. One bole
Was straight and single, another
A couple relaxed at a cocktail party, a third
A ménage à trois (quite comfortable), a fourth,
Fifth, sixth, and seventh a loving or warring
Crossing and conjoining of enormous limbs. Through the grid
The cajeputs are wrapped below, stellar
Above, palaestral below, adagio above, earthy
Below, airy above, fleshly
Below, spirit above, at last
Shadow below, sunlight above,
White shade, green-gilded sun.
We walked along the path, along the path, along
The line of cajeputs in their attitudes.

7. *Sky*

I admit it. This flat land
Supports a lot of sky. The road
Is stretched out like a tape measure, inched along

At the rush hour, lined with white cubes,
Gold cubes, pink cubes, cubes of powder blue,
With Australian pine, pandanus, palm, and poinciana.

Otherwise, sky. Similarly,
Over the bay. You walk down the lawn
Past the live oaks, the banyan, the gumbo limbo,

The two sedate date palms, the solemn
Avenue of royal palms, to where the last
Lone coconut palm leans out insouciant over the water.

Whitely the egret steps fastidiously by.
Blackly the cormorant spreads his wings to dry.
On a pole the pelican yawns an enormous brown yawn

Above the pink and blue endless ripple.
Blast that airplane, and that, and that.
But how did I get here?

The boom and buzz of this great bee
Through the sky. Bright blossoms of stars
Are still very distant. The sky
Is still very distant. It stands apart,
Holding its flowers. O tell me, Fleurdefeu,
How did we get here? The yellow grass,
The diminishing city, the small silver boxes,
The gray mist, the white mist,
The burst into blue above the white beach,
White desert, white vaporous ocean,
White monstrous snowfather. Dazzle
Beams up from the back of the cloud mass, not
From the higher, unlined, elemental face
Still gazing down from wherever its owner
Has backed off to. The clouds, says the man in the moon,
Are part of the earth. And I see the streaming black locks
Of your vaunted heaven. Which still gapes down
From wherever . . . O tell me, Fleurdefeu,
How cold is it here, how strong is the wind,
How thin is the air? Through the interference
Of double panes, the static of plastic and glass,
The monoscopic reception, I catch
A far sky, a flat sky,
A painted sky. Skies like trees

Blunt in paintings. But this scene is crayoned
In kindergarten: at the lower edge
Of the page, the strip of brown; at the upper edge
Of the paper, the stripe of blue; in the blank between,
Our silvery flight. Our shadow winged
Across the tops of the clouds, but the clouds are gone.
The dazzle is gone. We can stare out up
At the upper air. We peer down at Cape Fear,
Sharp, unmistakable, mapped, a mark.
The movie comes on. Please draw the blinds.
Next, stars glint far above and below
Our starless sail. To a gazer in a starry window
Below, our wingtips twinkle. Wherever we are
Is starless. We're held in the arms of the sky,
At arm's length, the face of the sky
Where it always was. We're sitting apart
Holding our arms, holding our flowers.

We flew east into sunrise through the night.
We flew south into summer through December.
Spring began again and again as we leapt northward.
We flew west from June and landed on January ice.
We captured miles of years in a glance from heaven.
Hibiscus by a white wall in this hot sun;
The distant recognized white straight gleam
Of the World Trade Center two inches high;
The bright, blue, cold Januarial sky
Behind the winter-lit branches.
The blue nuthatches, the chickadees, the creepers hold the trunks.
The juncos, the cardinals, the blue jays win the boughs.
The stiff gray alate beast drones its mastery over the air.
Epiphany is blue and clear. The first cracks show
In the armor of the witchhazel. Visible on the frozen pond
Are fallen leaves, thrown rocks, cracked sky.

8. Tree

The American elk and the American elm
Both have foreign names which suit them
Well enough, if, indeed, to the Proto-Indo-Europeans
Jabbering away in their smoky huts
During cold Caucasian winters, el
Meant red or brown. To the Proto-Indo-Americans
It was the white spot on their elk that mattered,
That gave it a name. Wapiti, they called it.
It wasn't an elk, of course, but a deer.
Their elk they called moose. Their deer
Someone dreaming of home named elk.
And what mattered on their elm?

February. The shadow seen.
Some white spots seen
Along the brown ridges of the elm.
The bold, barren shadow is stretched
Along the red bricks of the temple.

The shadow slips by.
No time for watching.
Short days. A short month. A short
Shadow. A short, cold time.

The grammar of winter is scratched
In diagrams. A squirrel is sucking
Icicles. Branches are adjectives ascribed
To the sky. Up there a squirrel is munching
Twiglets. The invention of the elm,
However, releases a rhetoric.
There's a Helen here, a Heracles here,
Beyond the unfluted columns, the flat
Metopes, the empty pediment.
Cassandra's wild arms rise as cries
Flash under gold guttae — the golden drops.
Apollo bends, turning tips to gold.

Reason

Reason meets dream.
Lines are persuasion.

If it weren't February it would
Be March. In no month in no year
Osiris was born.
The buds are bigger.
The periods soon will be commas,
Semicolons, question marks, shoots
Of exclamation.

In the temple, for the image of the god,
Stands a bowl of flowers resembling
The branches of the elk,
The antlers of the elm.

9. *Season*

I would not think of committing
The pathetic fallacy. I would not think
Of thinking the impluviation
Of the second day of spring
Was a sign (either symbol or symptom)
Of cloudy things about the heart
And behind the eyes or of what those clouds

Could do, she thought with a dim, dull thought,
Unstormily, without precipitation.
If the sun had smiled she might have had to weep.
But even when the rain stopped gilding the yellow grass
All the slivered crocuses flinched
As a wind circled loud as a plane,
Now in an attempt to land,
Now with an intent to bomb.
A few white pellets,
A few garnet-blossomed silver boughs
Began the bombardment. Landed,
That wind, automobilized, dashed
Through every red light.
Yesterday it was different.

Spring was her Achilles' heel,
She thought, clicking the cliché
Along the sidewalk. Higher heels
Are in again. Click, click. Cliché.
Achilles' heel. Hero
She was none, but well she knew
That once you've crossed the Rubicon
Each and every victory must be Pyrrhic
Except the last. Achilles' heel:
A double pain. They always get you in the spring.
Once Thetis or the obstetrician held you
With thumb and finger like tongs,
Dipping you, except for two small spots,
Into Stygian life. They always get you in the spring:
Alexander or Apollo,
Scylla or Charybdis,
The devil or the deep blue sea.

They sing you a siren song.
They offer you Pandora's box.
They turn down a Procrustean bed for you.
You can't turn it down.

She looked at the Procrustean bed.
Embroidered in pink on the pillow she read:
Get your act together. She found it odd
To be embroidered

Though the thread did not seem to be dangling much
From the needling words.

She looked into Pandora's box.
A bird cheeped: Hopefully, the sky at equinox
Can also be unlocked. The hopeful one
Had a sinking feeling

Though happily, presumably, most fortunately the sky
Was not yet falling.

She looked from where she was afloat
To where they sang. She rocked the boat.

Was

Was she so clever, had she such friends,
That she'd stay and cling

Though the call came ever clearer: Come
To us and sing?

Apollo, sunny singer, my destroyer,
Feverish whirlpool, deepest sea,
And what they will not believe.
I cannot make them believe
That march of the god
Through the march of March:
The enraged leonine entrance
To the witchhazel's re-clenched fists
That had sunnily spread benediction with incense
Above the late snow before the late frosts
(The epitaph of the crocus said:
Born in February, died in March —
A brief cold life in a trap of the sun);
Then the cardinal's cheering, the woodpecker's drumming,
The crow's crowing as he shook his black cloak
From the whitish summit of the sycamore
(Coming, coming, coming through the cold);
The reopening, the second crocuses,
The glints of green in the yellow grass
(Waiting, waiting, waiting for April);
The March snow sweeping
Along the black street,
The blue snow sleeping
Beneath the black trees;
Sun, an open window, beyond the traffic
A call: Phoebe, phoebe — not to the moon,
To the song of Phoebus, Phoebean aoedé,
La chanson
D'Apollon
Que nous écoutons.
Spring-resonant, sun-resplendent, the cardinal high in the maple,
A sheer incarnadine against sheer blue,
Flaunts our triumph over winter.

Winter is always with us.
Winter lurks in the spring:
Get and store,
Look aft and fore,
There's a monster soon,
There's a devil at noon,
To gulp your tune.
Watch the wintry arrow of the springborn Alexander.

Man or god will get you in the spring.
You may sacrifice the sun to entrenched and heroic grubbing,
You may sacrifice your fruit to eternal divine floration,
Between the devil and the deep blue sky.

The mockingbird sang through the rain.
The robin sang in an outburst of ruddy sun.

Not a red-breasted robin at all;
A deceiving American migratory thrush.
Shall I migrate, muse,

To hear the nightingale this spring,
To watch the wing-sweet swan,
To rent a windowed room? There's a vacancy
Among the lower Parnassian rocks.

10. Temple

In this room the clock has stopped.
Its silent face reflects like a moon.
A floral design in the carpet
Reflects designs beyond the bay window:
Flowers, stars. A full-faced moon,
As we sat all night under rough red blankets,
Accompanied our unresting flight toward dawn
With a constant gaze through the little curve of the window
And with, as though from the ocean, an answering
Gleam like perfume from the unflowered, unstarred carpet beyond the
    window,
                                                                    The

The old gray rumpled blanket of cloud below us.
The clock has stopped. Out in the garden
The old cat lies among the flowers
That last as the June days last,
As the blackbird's utterance lasts and lasts
Among the jewelled lilacs, over the glistering golden
Fleece of laburnum, along the stone walls. From the golden beak
The song flows, ripples, eddies, crashes on the rocks.
Through the splashes, through the flaps,
The wings of the swan ring over the silver waters.
Blue drops of speedwell bloom on the bank.
A northern island, Flora thought, is the land of flowers,
Indigo, violet, red, orange, gold, in a June of green
Freshened by the faithful clouds. Yet, Fleurdeleau,
The sun is reaching with a very long arm around the curve of the world.

O fortunate.

The wapiti now is nearly extinct
Over much of the United States. Before
The decline of the American elm its boughs
Were selected as sites for well-woven nests
By New World northern orioles — not
Orioles, of course, and yet
Clear goldfish of the American sky.

O lucky one
Who has begun.

In a land of orioles and lilacs —
Orange and lavender, sweet and clear —
She followed the scent of lilacs,
She followed the oriole call through the afternoon,
The flagrant flash through the afternoon sun,
On and on, moving on and on.
As the lavenders glistened into dusk,

Lavenders

Lavenders pure or lush or ethereal —
Lilac bush, wistaria vine, and princess tree —
She attended the woodthrush song through the evening,
The subtle invitation spaced with silence,
From a dark thicket, summoning to night.

O fortunate few
Whose walls are new
Under skies of blue.

The loud clock in the back room can be moved.
Now there is only the soft ticking of rain
And medium ticking of sparrows, with blackbird chimes.
The door is open into the back garden.
Traffic buzzes now and then, remote and weak.
In the strong house of stone — not clapboard, not brick — no radiator emits
Geysers toward a flaking ceiling
Or sprinkles a warped wooden floor.
She is not hastily moving clay tablets;
The showers fall outside. She buttons her red sweater.
The door is open to let in a little warmth,
But she is not looking out into the garden
And jumps up only to re-route a wasp.
A tablet lies under her hand. Where she looks
No color exists unless for an instant
The dull red wool. This is the unclocked time
To hear the involutions of the deep red rose of thunder.

Edging the thunder, entering the rose,
Slipping to the center of the burning woodthrush phrase,
Without a movement, in a rest wrung from movement,
Like the rest between two phrases —
Sometimes it is easy,
Sometimes it is impossible,
Sometimes it is meaningless. The meaning
Is there and is not there. For example,

The swan floats into the sunset.
The meaning floats far into the sunset
Before the thoughts, before the words,
Before the syllables are launched.
There at the edge of meaning he swerves.
If he should turn, return, storm
The still waters, fly
For her mind, she might glide
Out to the red sun, attain the thunder,
Enter. She did. She heard
The meaning. The woodthrush phrase
Curved around her. She
Curved around it. She could
Feel, like a wizened thin-fingered crone,
Among the rosy involutions; she could
Slide, like an eager rose-cheeked child,
To focus. Ah: the syllable
First said by the infant, last made
By the old aphasiac, solely sung
In the concerto for coloratura soprano
And orchestra. Keu: part of the ancestral
Word. Hear: part of the thought
Within the petals of the song.

If you were painting the three blatant oranges in the glass dish
Each would be daubed with a region of sunlit peaks
And shaded beyond the terminator. Within the crystalline ellipse
You would chart degrees, discover poles,
Fix the dark curve of one sphere on another.
If you surveyed the reiterated flowers on the papered wall
You would measure the cloud, the hour, the damascene
Angle painting and repainting
Petals brighter and darker than their orange centers.

Desire has its intonations. Do you remember
The orange and black of the oriole's imperative,
The orange sun at the heart of the sleek black tulip,
The sweep of the vast orange slide
On undulant meadows of lawn
Somewhere not far from the ocean
In the darkening of an August night?
That was the unmapped place
To desire the apricot sunning on the blackened bough
When from the blackened heavens
The constellations were calling.

The words of that sidereal call
Shone sharp and clear. But when you began
To transcribe them from a page of sky
You could not scratch so deep as they were high.
Oh: the longing of November wind.
Sweid: the swish of the leafy stars.
Desire: the valley and the hill.

Past the firebush,
Cornered by purple and gold I stopped.
Here I found it.

The slope seemed a bit unpropitious
And the big laburnum tree leaned so far
That the gardeners had reined it to the hillside.
But glimpsed behind the atropunic beech
Or watched from by the aurifoliate privet
The laburnum reared, gold tassels tossing,
Over the lavender breakers of rhododendron.
And so I cut my trapezoid through the air,
Posting at its unquestionable fines
Bush and tree and bush and tree,
Golden, purple, purple, gold,
Gold and purple leaves,
Purple and golden flowers.

Tesk and temple be before me.

                              Bounded by words
It had risen through the numinous mist
Waiting for contemplation, waiting for golden
Eagles to quarter the hillside, soar,
Soar, glide. Sheer rays of sun
Shone above the puffed purpureal clouds
As the great laburnum king above
The regal rhododendron. Free
From tint of red, both multitudinous
Lemon rods and lavender spheres
Pursued, like fixed stars, once the wind
Had rested, their unmoving course
Across the afternoon, beyond
The bright gleams of the privet,
The dark glints of the beech.
A golden mouth was moving in the tree,
A purple throat was moving by the bush.

Tem: The big fish cuts like a golden sword
Through the reflection of the purple iris.
Contemplate: The waiting iris shines
Unmoved above the mirroring pool.

When you looked from the large central window
Or opened the strong iron gate
You would glance at the small blue flower on the small white rock
And think that tomorrow,
And think that when the sky turned white and blue
You would burst into the sapphire of the morning
To view the flower on the rock.
Tomorrow a gray wind swooped from an old gray sky,
Or was it the old gray cat,
Or the old gray gentleman with his scythe?
The flower lay below the rock.

When you brought the little thing into the front parlor
You could see five-petaled perfection in the thimble of water
And remember the blue gaze gazing south from the rock
As you hurried from breakfast,

                                                                And

And remember forget-me-nots sprinkled by the swan-suave lake
As you ran to lunch,
And remember the Arabian swirl of blue smoke
Of ceanothus on the daisied hillside
As you rushed to supper,
And remember Dad's smooth hands in the funeral parlor.

An actual temple in a remembered sky:
This is possible. You can sow
White virgin columns in the rock
Below that clear blue. Wid: see.
Weid: have seen and know.
View: if not then, why not now?

Like the round head of a pin
Or a small seed above the rock
Yesterday the lithospermum
Bud gleamed hard and green,
As she stooped, in the little garden. In a vast garden,
The day before, in a northern Athens, the Himalayan
Deodar, like a green-feathered eagle, like a green-shagged peak
Gleamed, as she sat, with a distant misty Parthenon under its wing.

This is not our music. Ours,
Of more than spears that wing over mountains,
Of broken nuclei, trodden moons,
Beeps, crackles, tleers, and zooms.
Pandora's little hope
Goes up in smoke.

Where there is no affirmation
There are no lies. The bud softened.
The deodar poised like a deer
Or like a kitten that she wanted to stroke.
The moon above the Himalayas
Gleamed. The misty north sky darkened.
The lightning spared the tree.
She ran indoors and turned the key
And watched the storm through glass and spoke:

                                                                  Deru:

Deru: the acorn and the oak.
Doru: strength stronger than the spear.
Trust: if not there, why not here?

O lucky one
Who has begun
To build in the sun.

The only tree was the telephone pole
With its branches, the oversized bridge
Of the vast violin strung above the long arm
Of the street and bowed by the resident
Sparrow: Hear me, hear me, hear me,
Outside the grayish window
Of the brick apartment house. Hello,
Hello. Hear me, hear me.

O fortunate few
Whose walls are new.

The bees buzzed back, officially announcing
A universe no longer ananthous.
It was time to do her tenth symphony
In the vowelless syllables of Bella Coola.
Green grass, one week miraculous,
The next week was taken for granted.
It was time for temples, epics, festivals,
Lawns and lawnmowers,
Leaves and the shadows of leaves.
A fragrance in a stray wind
Was of the scents that are remembrances:
Evenings of robin and apple blossom,
The forbidden beauty of the rosebud cherry,
Innocent as a child's kisses.
The breeze flowed through the bars
Of the fire escape. O Fleurdefeu,
                                            Tell

Tell her it is time to solmizate
April's orange elms,
May's pink oaks,

The vibrant white of dogwood on dark
Hemlock. The innocent breeze
Went whispering down the lanes,
Was pushed down narrow lanes between
Skyscrapers. Prohibited strains
Seeped from the short American spring.
But during the expanding afternoon
Below the silver maple's bloody flowers
She had drowned in the deep blue squills.

O luck.

The little clock is ticking. The wind
Calls Wish in the leaves and Want in the chimney.
Ears are lidless. At the sharp gray peak
Of the Empire State Building when it was Everest
Of buildings, wind suspired thus, circling
Auricularly yet not sweeping
Eyeglasses upstream or out to sea.
See, the river unwinds north,
The ocean unfolds into daybreaks. Go
As the wind goes. The old red blanket
Billows on the slats. Liftoff. Everest.
Evenings of green, rose, marble,
Eagles, skies, evenings of skies.

11. *Season*

At midnight we walked out toward the sea,
Leaving our teacups beside the peat fire.
The silvery ground of the sky
Displayed some orange and purple tracks
Left by the scarlet slug that had slipped into the north.

Two

Two shadows circled sirening
Gently. We blinked at the striking
Of giant matches on headlands and islands.
From glinting tracks the endless train
Of the sea kept sounding.
We pulled our winter coats tighter.
It was summer.

Behind us, to the east, was the hill
We climbed from the little road.
Three thousand years before, feet
Climbed the hillock, eyes
Measured the rows, firm hands
Held the slabs straight, patted the stones
Against each base, where the tormentil
Glittered gold beneath the circling
Curlew, circling lapwing, plunging
Lark, above dark purple orchids
And the lavender antlers of the ragged robin,
Above misty towers of cathedrals of the sea,
The antlers of two oil rigs. The wind came circling
Around the gray sky and plunged
Upon the cows, upon two homines sapientes standing
Between the Bronze and Petroleum Ages.

The stone rows in the grass above the North Sea
Resembled a graveyard above Narragansett Bay,
Without inscription, without Dad's date, without Dad's name.

Behind us, to the west, was the hill
We climbed from the little road.
It was bigger, and the path we tried
Was the path of a spring. When we reached the top,
Stopping for eyebright, walking among
The tormentil, hearing the curlew and the lark,
Seeing the sheep and the fields, rising above
The grassy stony mounds of the men who gave crops to the north
And chambered tombs to themselves five thousand years before,
We discovered, sharp and clear, beyond the fields, beside the sea,
Two white shapes:
                                                  A visiting,

A visiting, naturalized, geometrized moon,
The great white gleaming smokeless sphere
Of (already old-fashioned, outmoded, out-of-date)
The experimental fast reactor (DFR),
And beside it, issuing cloud-white draconic breath,
An anatural, geometrical, anthropometrical chunk of the globe of space,
The great white gleaming smoking solid rectangle
Of (still forerunner, still of the future, still of the about-to-be)
The prototype fast reactor (PFR).
We crossed the cairns, two bipeds stepping
From the New Stone to the Nu Clear Age.

These days never gave up their ghosts.
Silvery spirits hovered, tinged
With orange and purple, about their lips.

12. *Tree*

How can she remember it now —
With the blinds down, with the movie on, with the smoke drifting back,
With the intermittent clatter at the bar, with the constant
Oom of the engine, far above
The clatter and oom of the ocean,
The blinding cinematic clouds —
How in the quiet forest garden where the goldcrest fluttered
The green Caucasian fir
Pulled at the muscles of her eyes?
It was a perfect triangle, shining green, light-tipped
But dark within, pulling her eyes
Wider and wider.

13. *Sky*

The greenish-yellow candles of ailanthus
Lit in a gray July.
The heat of the sun without the sun,
The moisture of rain without any rain,
Encased and lined her. Sticky,

                                                          Succinctly

Succinctly reported the announcer.
And it was linden time. The rare
Breezelets sweetened segments of atmosphere
On the lee shore, where she wished
To be found, to be. The ailanthus
Nestled against the brick wall.

The golden candles of the rain tree
Lit the garden. Still the opaque
Gray plane of sky resisted contemplation,
Smashed the yo-yo of her vision,
Letting her almost hear the clack
Of the gray painted billboard, the clang
Of iron, the thunder over rain.

When the rainbow stretched down over the grass
She almost ran to the foot of the mountain.
Yet it was on a February afternoon,
Without grass, without mountains, without rainbows,
That she sighted the keystone of the heavens.
All the horizons were pale, but straight up, above the elm,
Smoldered that blue,
Not pale, not dark, not dull, not bright,
But deep, receptive, penetrable,
The vertex once known.
Banish the restlessness of adjectives to rest
In the temple, sink into the sky,
And kiss the light.

And here it is on the fourth of July,
Squeezed out between the leaves,
Or smeared, as she leans on the black railing,
There over the roof of the brick building
Where a single swift flits swerving,
Or sampled as a river between two elms
With a bay beyond and then an ocean
Where white fleets pass and are gone,
And the green banks of elm leaves approach her and sharpen —
The banks move while the river is still —

And

And the blue supernal river deepens in its channel
And, flowing green over grass between shores of shadow,
Deepens as her eyes cleave the earth
(If these — they must be, though not unmistakably — are
What that February sky, although unmistakably, was),
Or sensed — this is it — with the windows pushed up, the shades drawn
    over the panes,
The world seen, heard, and felt through the screens,
In the room's three-quarter summer light,
Close, here, on the books, on the chair, on the floor,
As a sparrow harps, as a bicycle fiddles,
As an airplane croons, as a bus sighs: You
Could join this light
Without parades, without firecrackers, without loud adjectivals.
Even the nouns and the verbs have begun to disappear,
Leaving infinitives.

                N'y voir que du bleu?
Of course, there are certain predications
Sweetly breathed from the gold and purple throat
Of the fair catalpa, allegedly made
By the bittersweet nightshade of purple locks
And pointed golden tongue.
The bricks are fire-baked.
The samaras are flames.
The tree of heaven is smoke-resistant.
This sky is the empyrean.
Whether it is the sky or some eagle beating
In herself or, shadowed among the sand dunes, herself,
With the shore lost, with the sun lost,
With the wet grass knifing her knees,
This fire goes on burning.
Here is an escape.

The Sheen

1. *Troy*

Apart. Where the gold.
At lunch. O forget it.
But that's. Well, not now.
The issues. Not now.
Apart, where the gold-lined wings
Were actions, were wings of words
Louder than actions, were silences
Louder than words, she sat
In the afternoon's deserted field
By the edge of the thicket. In the trees
Bronze birds with gold-lined wings
Were sometimes leaves, were sometimes
What they were. The leaves flickered.

Bronze and gold, the words fluttered
Into mown autumn. At lunch.
Forget it. Not those words. Silence
Dappled the grass. Apart.
The aspen crowds were cheering, waving
Their hands, their handkerchiefs, jingling coins
In their pockets. Fire-engine cardinals
Broke for the scarlet camouflage now
Proffered by the euonymus. The Ionian white and gold
Of the birches lined the portico. Apart.
She couldn't work anyway, with all that noise
From the maple. The archangelic sky
Trumpeted out of its distances pure
Blue glories. Not allowed.

Prohibited: one golden glimpse
Without that, there, or then.
One golden glimpse. Finding a camp chair,
She dragged it over. Here was the sky,
Here the maple, here the grass
Filling again with robins, here
The wood, and here the hill.

Up the hill someone was painting
A poignancy of red, the aureolation of orange,
Those kingly purples, on a green canvas.
Let it be something manly, Jack,
Something virile, something of authentic virtue,
Not these ecstasies of autumn, sunset,
Triple rainbows beyond the ridge,
Waning slices of moon beyond
The birches. And yet ascent
Is easiest. How your moccasined feet
Lope up the rocks while your eyes deny
All but crest and sky.
Your toes are pinched, your knees out of joint
As you slouch back down. I paint what I see
And always in natural light, with gloves
If needed: hues, tunes, weathers,
Tints, shades, shadows,
Shadows, caverns as of clouds,
De profundis surfaces,
Surfaces, species. A breeze
Sent gold and crimson leaves like fallen angels in facile ascent
Toward their old places on high.

You can't see it? It was surfaces she loved,
Yet she hovered at edges, which suggested depths
Without requiring penetration. The irrelevant
Butterflies glittered near her in the field;
Flashing significance, the flickers flicked
At the tips of the thicket. Meanings like those
Of a green island in a stream,
Of a white island in an ocean,
Reached

Reached her eyes as she sat in the enormous clearing
Watching, to the cicadas' orchestration,
Past the goldenrod and Queen Anne's lace,
The stage where action glimmered among the columns of the trees.
There's something there.
But under the klieg afternoon
All the birds stopped playing their parts.

One golden glimpse. She turned to the maple.
Here was perfect surface and sure
Dimension curving behind the facade.
The sextant of her gaze
Adjusted to the shock of scarlet
And all the orpiments. She recognized
The tones of reality, away
From the usual unreal. She understood
The parallax of reality, apart
From the real club sandwiches, headlines, companionate

Mutterings. She gobbled the communion.
Far from the cry of battle and the rhetoric of the assembly
Where men reel in glory she listened
To messages other than the shadows, as the gold-tongued maple
Spoke, with undertones of viridity,
With overtones of bronze bells clanging,
In releasing rhythms, of angles
Of satisfaction: slanting
Panting almost, sharp red now,
And coppery reflection; the climb, the top,
The symphony in the resounding valley,
Mosaics for them to walk on, to dig up,
To reconstruct; matter only
Holding form, only emitting
Energy, only accepting
The ears' fierce grasp,
The eyes' slow fiery osculation.

Because it was quite enough
Or because it was not quite enough,
The intersection of tree and sky
Seemed the clearest clear, the truest
Gold, the happiest blue. And wading out
From the bright strand into the bright
Azure she began to feel
On ankles, on thighs, on shoulders the eternal
Swirl, the eternal pull.
Is there a tide in the sky?
Is there an undertow in the sky?

No, you can't say these things.
You can't say any of these things.
But what were they saying at lunch? You've got
To do something? Actions, they said.
Well, you know that women weigh less
On pay scales. Gosh, two nights in a row?
Well, just a scare. You know
That women are night's booty. But what
Did they say he said? Well, words
Will never. Apart. Where the gold.

Down the blue Kennebec we came,
Pushing our way around the rocks
Before we could pack the water into dams,
The soil under rails, the soil into lanes
For thruways, the soil into strips
Under airways. Up the brown Kennebec we flew.

The sun set, and the saints' dark bodies
Stepped up into the light, stood
In the glass. From the dark she saw them.

The green and yellow and orange translucent
Around them, sectioned, simpler than the deepening
Darkening sunset of the maple,

Gave them their own plainer, flatter,
Not less luminous, more enduring
October as an environment

In which their stance, solemn, almost
Opaque, was inviting, promised the high
White wax aflame —

Peaks of radiance, flowing and rippling
Rivers of song, mists as sweet
As ten June evenings, and, sweeter,

The secret taste of God on the tongue,
Down the throat, in the breast. Then all heads bowed.
Heavy the incense hung.

We made it here on that eighteen-seater
That tosses you over and over the billows of air,
Or stacked our stuff in a U-Haul and tugged
It up in spite of five hours gasped second
By second across the George Washington Bridge,
Or survived the unventilated hold of the Greyhound bus
Becalmed before clearing Boston.

Turning away, she walked down apart from the clutter of people
By the white sea foam, looking out over the wine-shaded deepness,
Praying aloud, with her hands stretched over the glittering water.
Far in the distance the four white ships went on sailing together.

Across the lake the four white swans sailed on
In smooth and silent beauty. Yet one smashed
Against that yielding element: he crashed
His forces on the surface; splashed great sprays
Into receptive air; in might was gone,
Received along the singing, flashing ways.

Across the pond the four white ducks
Progressed in order, by mute rules
And uttered regulations. Grass,
For her the last solidity,
Had launched them. From the dry and firm
Terrestrial slope her arms reached forth
Above the level, yielding, stirring
Spread. The steeple rippled down.

That bounded, unending liquidity, where her steps stopped,
That alien pliancy past the margin where she walked
Shadowed itself brightly on the tree trunks, where the light
Flexed. Like long-haired Achaeans, the willows
Stood strong and comely. Like gods, the willows
Swished their silver ambrosial locks, turned gold
As the chryselephantine anatids sank on the gilded hill.
And from where the fowl had been laboring on the shore
A hundred swans, a thousand gleaming ships
Crossed the wide water, prows forward, sails proud,
To be beached among the bottles. Dotted
With gold the warblers darted out.

Catch a bug.
Catch a fish.
Catch a god.
Like an anhinga, the warbler
Was shaking his wetted wings.

The silvery willows reached out, touching
The silvery waters. The watery willows
Reached the willowy waters. The silvery
Surfaces touched. The willowy silvers
Met the silvery willows. The watery
Silvery willows met the waters.
The surfaces touched. And Flora knew,
When the ducks stopped gossiping, how easy it would be
For someone sitting by a gray-bearded father,
Someone willowy, watery, silvery,
Someone silver-footed swiftly to plunge
Up from the sunken inverted weather-vane ship.

The pond went rushing with the wind
Faster and faster to the inevitable edge.
A silvery chill came gliding across the water,
Insinuating eld into the gray beards of the willows.
The wind blew up a cerulean ocean
Lined with the repetitive signposts of the trees.
Down upon the ducks came floating

Feathers of the firstling snow.
What weathercock trees.
The elegant willowy tresses have thinned.
She's walking on hairs.
They crackle, as the ducks crackle, on the grass.
They lie by the duckless pond in the soundless snow.
When were the sails unfurled?
When were the oars pushed down?
Beyond the yellowish, diminished willows
The still, thick pond is obdurate. The frozen ripples
Never shift. No one now will get through.
There, testing the ice, stands a gull
That has beaten in from the distant ocean.

2. Ithaca

Neither stay-at-home Penelope
Nor cute little Nausicaa
Nor that bitch Calypso
Nor Helen at forty playing the gracious hostess
Back in Sparta with her starry-eyed husband
Nor sister Clytemnestra the killer
Nor certainly Circe for all her aplomb
But the Muse-sung male was her hero:
The role-model, the archetype, the star.
Male me in tell Muse much turning.
What hero ever stayed at home
Or, like Nausicaa, did the wash
At an outdoor laundromat or crazed
Men into bestiality? Tell me, Muse,
What do you think?

When there was no longer a pond
But only a white slope and a white plain
And the wind built a white mountain on the plain
And a hand planted a stick on the mountain
Like an oar to Neptune, it was time to depart.

A numb hand clutched the handle of her tote bag full of books.
She was stepping down the white hill like an egret wearing boots.
Nevertheless, when she reached the bridge,
She saw him/her as he/she stood
Backed by black pines, white birches, gray alders
On a white shore beside the black waters.
Seek past gray but never suppose

There is only the beachhead where you stand or only
An elusive current coursing through night.
The moon rustled in the stream.
The dry snow shone.

Down the white Kennebec she flew,
Then between flights slid into a cab
And skidded off to check some footnotes.
Then, as the elevator redescended, there he was
In his soft gray suit. Hi! Which way? Down.
Which way were they going? The cage
Dropped quickly around her heart.
His gray locks shocked her. They were thick, though,
And his gray eyes electric. Then they stared
At his glistening boots and her sodden loafers.
Time for a cup of coffee? No. But thanks.
The wet snow hung heavy on the yews.
A gray squirrel clung to the garbage basket grate.
She cleared the slush. The taxi splashed off.

Then they were spraying the smoking icy wings.
Then. Then. Then. The bump,
The braked run, the stiff stumbling
Walk, the dizzying watch, the turning
Luggage, thump. Then the warm
Moist breeze, the green, the green.

Sun showered the umbrella tree
And dripped from its glistening domes
As frisbees whirled like discuses
And happy voices called her in.
Here's the bath, and here's the feast,
And here are our newest songs.
Tell us now about your trip.

I shouldn't have said that
About Calypso. She was kind to me.
But she wanted me to forget
The fires blue burning above
My Ithaca. Her soft
Words, her soft . . . But this is the end
Of my story.

        The beginning?

From the bay their four white arms
Kept flashing as they swam to the green
Slope of the lawn. Did they see me
As I sat by a palm tree that rattled
Like raindrops rattling on a roof?

Above the roof the vultures'
Black and sun-tan wings
Sidled closer and closer, but wind
Filled with sun was sweeping sweetly
Across the green. The wind was a sea
In the shells of my ears as I stood up and walked
On the stubbly grass, on the spongy grass.
There was no grassy grass. The pelicans
Flopped, the palm feathers flapped, the pelicans
Flipped, the palm fingers clicked.
The squeaks of the gulls, the bray of the jay,
The protestations of the parrot
Greeted the singers singing on the shore.
The wind whispered across the water.
The sun screamed across the water.

As far away the sun is playing
His icicle lyre, so the wind here fingers
The harpstrings of the palm, they sang,
And we sing to you. Female, woman,
We will not break you on the rocks where the bones
Whiten in the sun. Those are men's bones.
Woman, female, with us you will sing
On the grass among the purples of the butterfly trees.

The fish were swimming in the air,
The birds were flying under water,
The plants were spreading their sails,
I was taking root. The roots of the trees
Swung and swayed in the burnishing breeze.
But I heard above and beyond the leas
The wet sound of the water,
The dry sound of the palm.

Does the wind have a sound of its own?

                                          We know
The words of the wind, the truth of the trees,
The questions of water, the answers
Uttered by the shore — the shore
Of Troy, of Lesbos, of Athens, of sandy
Pylos, of Ithaca. We know how to sing

These answers. Don't smear wax
On your ears. Don't tighten the bonds
That restrain you. Don't refuse
To listen. Don't be afraid to come.

Does the wind have a sound of its own or only
The cluck of the water, the clack of the palm?

A creek flowed into the bay.

Across the creek
The four white egrets
Did their thing.
Two sat in trees:
One hunched asleep,
The other preened.
Two walked the shore:
One stalked the slope,
The other, wetting
Big black boots
In wading kept
His white parts dry.

Along the creek browsed Australian pines,
Birch-bark cajeputs, and gray-plated
Earleaf acacias. The acacia flowers
Are golden caterpillars and their fruits
Bronze labyrinths where, on sharp orange hooks,
Black beads hang gleaming.
I put one labyrinth into my handbag
And crossed the gray concrete bridge.

Whether the egrets were men
I wasn't quite sure, but the pigs were.
The women, though, said Circe, I turn
Into schoolgirls, to whom I teach skills
They need in a pig-run world. But you,
Since something has shown you the labyrinth (for
When she waved the pointer I, long-schooled, did not shrink) —
You, too, will instruct them. The schoolroom was restless
Like a pen of navy-blue, white-collared calves,
With big bronze eyes turned outward. Groping
Along the bronze passages, I imparted the thread
Which I could hardly claim to descry:
How to fast, how to feast, how to speak, and how
To shut up. Around us we heard
The endless rooting and grunting.

An egret — a white cloud in his tree —
Suddenly started to scratch his ear.

When a red bird bloomed in the oleander
And a green bird flew shrieking down the creek
And a blue bird flashed up into the cajeput
And the egret's camel S stretched into an I,
Then Circe said: It's time for you to go.
The waterlight spun on the white barber poles
As I pushed off against the current.

Across
The pool
The four
White blos-
Soms swam.
Beside
The spar-
Kling wa-
Ter sat
Helen
In her ba-
Thing suit
With her cig-
Arette
In her tanned
Fingers.

Jack, too shy to hand them to her,
Had set the flowers afloat. Yes,
She was beautiful. Yes, she was
A worthy daughter of deep-browed Jupiter.
Yes, you would almost have to believe
What she was saying: And therefore the ERA
Will damage fragile balances erected
Through centuries by western civilization.
We defeated the Trojans, an Asiatic race,
And now, without fear from abroad,
If we maintain our defenses at home,

We

We can enjoy in peace our Hellenic blessings. Women—
I know, for I have sinned—are fitted by nature
For marriage and for religion. Let them make heaven
And take their husbands along. I must
Give up smoking. Extending her arm,
She stubbed out her cigarette. She stood up,
Stepped to the edge, tensed, waited poised,
And dived into the pool. The white
Blossoms bobbed about her in a frenzy.

My oars were gone, my boat was smashed,
But I crawled up onto the shore
At the foot of the long mild slope of the lawn.
After about an hour I limped up the grass
And hobbled along the straight gray drive
Lined by stone gray columns of royal palm.
I remember at the end two fruiting cycads
And two date palms on their rooty hills
And the heavy door being pushed open.

I awoke in a sunny bedroom, watching
The sun in the thick green figleaves,
The sun in the long green fingers,
The sun in the long gold fingers,
Of queen palms, the sun in pink lips
Puckered around red tongues
Of triple-flowered hibiscus, the sun
In the screens, in the slats, on the sheet,
On her gray silk blouse. She looked anxious, then relieved.

Except for the three brawny maids who spoke
A language of unfamiliar intonation and refused
To raise their eyes even to my chin,
She was the only person on that island,
I found as I explored
Among its breezes. Golden gleams
In the scarlet threads of the callistemon,
Skyflowers, coral vines, queen's wreaths, flame vines
Found me. When I was well

                                                      And

And ready to say goodby, she interrupted:
Though I'm called Calypso, I will not hide
My thoughts. She took my hand
And drew it slowly between soft breasts.
Stay here, she said, and touched the top button
Of her sleek silk blouse. The rosy-lipped,
Red-velvet-tongued hibiscuses
Nodded by the hot white wall.
But as soon as Mercury descended
In his hydroplane, she let me go.

The Phaeacians smiled. The sun
Slanted like sleet through the slats
Of the jalousie windows, along
The princess's flaxen hair. Remain
And teach good Greek to our daughter,
The queen invited. But if you can't,
Stay as long as you can. And if you must go,
We'll help you. Just give us your name and address.

My name is Flora Urania Baum. My home,
Which I seek, is Ithaca Island, on which stands
A mountain rich in trees and rainbow flowers
With summits rising far above the gray
Of rains and mists and clouds into the great
Blue binding of our black-cased world. I seek tall oaks
And polychromatic flowerets — gold crepe, crimson
Silk, peach satin, velvet prussian blue,
And lace of burnt sienna. I must read,
Then, the candid letters on the spine.

Stay as long as you can. But if you must go,
We'll send you in our silver Cadillac.

                                        Smooth,
So smooth was that ride she awoke
Only at sunset near the bridge
Beyond the gray strait. What shall I say
Of the plow deep in the black earth,
Of the peak white against the sky?

                                             The

The sky bound her. In the clarity of that night
She knew its blackness and the whiteness of each star.
Violet-sweet through the dark flew the scent of each butterfly flower.
And out past the palm tree's castanets
The sun rose over the cove's cloud-marbled floor.

3. Delphi

It has been asked before:
Why would anyone's tears
Greet the golden columns and the rosy cliffs?

He was a Greek god.
Do you understand? He was a god.
He stood there in his divinity.

I know about gods. They're not all the same.
Some — but why enumerate?
He — how shall I explain?

It was on the first day of April
That I left the shore and the port and began
My walk up the stream. The peaks rose beyond.

He should be back. It's spring.
Though the narcissus is hard,
The hyacinth tightly bound,

Squills in bluest profusion
Have poured into the channels of twilight,
Deep with copiousness.

Open your eyes. Though no groves
Of olive shimmer silver, though
No laurel waits in perpetual green,

Aspens strung with gray and red,
Alders strung with bronze and gold,
Stand without impatience.

And though no gleaming swan
Oars him stately along,
Seven wingèd swimmers play.

See duck. See duck.
Be our beggars.
Run for our crusts.

The ducks are so amusing,
Being ducks, ducking,
Tipping up those curly tails.

The ducks are so loquacious,
Uttering their respective syllables:
Their long spondees, their tribrachs and tetrabrachs.

The ducks are civilized.
Observe, after her invitation and his acceptance,
The courtliness of their mutual bows.

A duck has his pride.
There goes aggressive Achilles,
Rebuffed, striding down the lawn, sailing from the dissatisfactions of
   Troy.

Far above us ducks
Strain with the strength of pinions
As they peer through the miles.

She laughed. I enjoy them, too.
Did you see how the big white one
Sailed down the stream like a clipper ship,

Fought, and, waked by victory, returned?
I suppose, I said, he's the ugly duck
Among the mallards. If not quite a swan,

Though big, he's not domestic,
Feral at least, ferocious at times,
Off on his high charger to the attack.

I resent, though, his bellicosity, his
Womanizing. Nature, she said.
The race must go on.

Her gray eyes sparkled, her armor shone.
Am I not my father's child?
Her eyes, like olive groves, glimmered.

And so I went on up.
Summits attract. What can you do
But climb? Your spirit flutters

Almost with wings. You will see
Where you were and where you were not,
Where you are and where you are not,

Where you could be. You will choose
Among the visions, among the beauties,
Among accessible things,

Among inaccessible things —
The hyacinth and the farthest hill,
The odoriferous blue, the remote

Smoky blue. The old green of pines
Guarded the young green of the birches.
The young fluid green was smeared

Across the fabric, mixed with sun
Dipped from the tulips' unemptying cups.
A pretty picture? The cups

Filled and refilled, red, yellow, mauve,
Red jewel, yellow lantern, mauve
(Deep dark mauve) solar spring.

I drank. A pretty picture?
There he stood. Was it frightening?
Behind him rose the columns and the rocks.

A Greek god is a statue,
Naked, powerful, and perfect,
Every muscle of his marble arm

In harmony. Cold ancient youth,
What have you to do with me perusing
Your body — that buttock, that knee,

That perfect accusing or caressing arm?
I accept that accusation and that caress,
I am forced to accept, I am forced

To feel sun reach through cloud,
Blaming the disaffection of the eye,
Claiming the flesh that glowed

When beyond the frame, beyond the panes,
The box elder burst into lambent green flames
And shuddered its way to gold.

A Greek god is an actor
In an old play. He stands on the roof
And speaks iambic. A girl

Runs across the circle, tearing
The wreath from her unleashed hair.
Cruel! To make me tell yet tell in vain!

A sobbing woman pulls
Her cloak yet tighter, shaking.
Cruel! When I did yield to kill the child!

(Hedged about by lilac, on the youthful grass,
Things soft and fierce,
The green glittering sundrops of the birch beyond.)

From the roof the mask delivers
Deep-voiced the measured reply.
Your son lives on. Your words live on. You die.

This does not die: the bubble and swirl of robin song in the dusk,
The tune of slim birch gleam in April dusk, the purple notes
That spurt from the soil where the unearthly

Hyacinth sits on the earth and sings
Deep full gathered multitudinous song
Ascending April nightfall.

A Greek god is a breath
That carries an echo of music
Breathed on your ear, on your mouth, you can't breathe,

You can't hear, you hear that music, you breathe
That echo, it rattles in your chest, your chest
Echoes, you know you can't breathe, there's something

On your lips, on your tongue. At dawn,
In the silences between the intonations,
Half awake, half asleep, you repeat,

As though you heard a language recorded,
With silences between the uttered phrases,
The phrases of the thrush from the wood above the gully.

Listening. Singing. Wait.
Singing. Nothing other. Singing.
Listening. Wait. Singing.

Come on into the wood, she said,
If that's your notion of divinity.
I'll show you the way. There were no paths.

That she could slip through keyholes
I knew as I tried to follow,
Bending under branches, barging

Through brambles, sliding along
The moss, into mud, running along
The verdant three-leaved ivy, among

The ardent triple-tongued mosquitoes. Were the birds
Leading or fleeing as they flitted just ahead,
Ever ahead in the shadows? Beyond

The velvet-padded zigzag fence,
The swimming hole's brocaded edge,
We came to the lyrical brook.

When born among the quivering trees
I did not weep but on the breeze
Began to sing.

I sang a philosophical song
Of earth and stars and right and wrong
And wondering.

I felt the soil, I watched the sky,
I entered roots, was entered by
Far-falling rain.

I plunged beneath the whirling world
And leapt with silver wings unfurled,
Hot to explain

All that I thought. I thought. I lay
Along the grass all summer day
Deep in the shade,

Deep in the sun, silent, then stirred.
He came. He thought. He sang. He heard.
He was afraid,

Envied my effort and my rest,
And kicked a stone upon my breast,
And changed my tune.

I sing, I speak, I think, he said,
But to my infants and my dead
Low you may croon.

From the stadium where the young men strip off their clothes
And run the long race to the west, then turn and return,
You can see the blue gulf

Blazing as Greek gulfs blaze, without strain, and the young
Men's effort seems effortless, too, so graceful are they,
Like the grace of blue flame.

If you climb in the other direction, toward the east,
Up the cliffs, you reach the chilly, dripping cave,
High on Parnassus yet sunk deep into the earth,

Where nymphs whisper and whistle and mortal women
Unbraid their long hair. From that rocky, watery cave
(Confer Pausanias) even a well-girt male

Must sweat to attain the top. It's a hard ascent
And the peaks are above the clouds and upon the peaks
Thyiades rave

To the god with drums, with flutes, with chants, with cries,
With cries in their women's voices, with human cries,
Beauty will save,

And run down, down, down,
Dizzy, dizzy, down, down,
Spinning, tumbling, down, down,

Past the goats, the springs, down,
Past the firs, the cave, down,
Past the theater, down, down,

By the temple rising tall,
By the high retaining wall,
By the statues that will fall,

By the pillared stoa fair,
By the treasure houses rare,
By the ruins lying there,

Past the angry Centaurs, down,
Past the three-man Geryon,
Past the fighting giants, on

Past the warring heroes, on
Past the battling Amazon,
Past the goddesses and ducks, down, down.

Out by Twelvemile Brook
Where blackbirds flash red wings
Sped Artemis.

Over the Messalonskee
Where flickers glitter toward the bridge
Strode Athena.

On toward Mayflower Hill
With the blue glint of the swallow
Strolled Apollo.

4. *Eleusis*

She's gone. The earth is white. The sky
Is black. Footprints on the snow
Tramp into shadow.

                    Did you think
When the leaves fell you would see
A gowned figure among the boles,
When the snow fell you would find
The light tracks across the plain,
When the night fell you would know
Her cry in the silence?

                All day
The chickadees called cold. Did you wait
Till the wind fell to ascend
The bitter hill? Did you turn
As you climbed to let the sun
Just for a moment feel your cheeks?
When the rain fell did you want
Ice to clench the earth? Did you say
No to the landscape? Did you say
No to the land?

                You must have clamped
Each hand around itself and pounded
Your chest, pressed your forehead, and knuckled
The cold sting of your tears. You stamped,
You ran against numbness into pain.
Your pain was a shout, a torch, a hound.
Was there a rush into your arms,
An answering "Mother, Mother"?

As you crossed the bridge you knew
Only your shadow was moving
On the white silence of the stream.

As you crossed the bridge you experienced
The gephyrism of the wind
Jeering. You hammered your ears.

As you crossed the bridge you bowed before
Vociferous sleet, mute swanlike winging snow.
The whishing, chugging motors of your feet
Driven down the dazzling lane
Reached the sonant fountains of the snowblowers
And dragged you to witness the agriculture of winter.
The snow is plowed and the frost blossoms.

                              But where is she?

Behind the flower stood
Death.

               How in a moment
Transitions are made — how the green and golden
Universe instantaneously dissolves
With the brief misplacement of a foot,
With a slight papery slice across an eye,
With a willed or unwilled word — needs no explanation.
We all live at the edge. But one
So young, so lovely, so immortal —
How could she surmise
In the plucking of a single bloom
As her small hand drew away the flower
That brute plucking? The sod cracked.
He leapt upon her.

                    She lives now
In a lifeless region, under the sown seed.

And why did her powerful father look the other way?
To men is granted power, to women
The bearing of power. Earth
Bore Sky; to mighty Sky,
Her child, she bore strong sons
Whom he hated and hid. But his son
Unmanned his father, wedded
The wife who bore strong sons
Whom he hated and hid. But his son . . .

How did it end? To Death
He gave his daughter. He let her
Be hidden in Earth. Somehow it worked.
His sons were clones, skylings
(The mother merely bears the father's
Seed, averred the Athenian justice,
And she a goddess), his daughter
Rose with spring, descended
With every fall.

               That went on a long time.

Now it's March in Maine. There's summer in the sun.
Between us and summer, between us and the sun
Extends a chilly atmosphere. Yet noon
Reaches through, exciting sweetness
In the pallid grass.

     And something new,
More than the dead duck floating down the stream,
Emerges as the green ice breaks.

       We've tried —
Learning what happened when you picked that narcissus —
We've tried very hard to find you, goddess,
Girl, last seen running through a field
All bloom. We pondered in the syllables of the wind
Consonants, vowels, or only vowels,
Yes or no or only eh
Or oh. We got the message, we read
The fable, winter. We held up pines
As torches, saying, See, they're green,
There's green. The snow quenched that. That white
Refutation undid our names. We crawled
Through blackest caverns, hoping that here,
Far from the snow-glare, deep in the dark,
Freed from trying to see, free
To feel, we would touch your skirt.

       From the earth,
As the yellow tips turn green,
And the green-enfolded pillars build,
And the green wraps hint of gold,
As the snowdrops rise and the snowdrops fall,
And the slush, of rose and silver,
Fades into the watery twilight, and in the dusk
The white duck is a moon
Moving down the stream, and through
The bearable night the stream goes flowing,
And as at dawn the gold and white and green
Plunge below the bank, pointing to the blue
            Center

Center of the globe, like torches pointing,
And are not reflections, in that clarity
Are true trees, willow, birch, and pine,

Among green blades the white and golden
Maiden issues with a tune in her throat,
Rises with a pen in her hand,
Singing her own song,
Writing her own account.

Between sterility and stability,
Between continuation and dissolution,
Between life and life, and death and death,
The crocuses come, the roses come,
The leaves redden, the boughs grow white,
The crocuses come. They are not the same.
Spring is back, they say, you say.
Spring is not back. Spring goes forever.

Oh, our lovely Persephone has returned.
Am I the same, when I have seen
(Down there, where I sit in brocade,
With a scepter in my lace-gloved hand)

Achilles weep, Agamemnon warn
Against all women, Odysseus at last
(Ulysses no longer) close his eyes
To questing, Penelope set her hand
At best to her shuttling, and the web
Of the universe wax and decay?

Pericles came by, Napoleon
Shuffled over, Hitler dropped in
Heavily, and in a corner
Sappho sat at her lyre.
There grew an eternal garden
With everlasting tumbling runnels
And apple blossoms fresh forever
And rest rustling from the leaves.

Who wants apples when the apple blossoms
Are fresh forever? We want bread
But we want roses and the rose
That does not die.

    Tithonus
Begged his end, and Sibyl prayed
Nine hundred years for instant death.

I have dropped my scepter, taken my pen,
And written what I saw as I ascended:
The splendid pallor of the grass,
The faint purple light of the crocus on the snow,
The dawn-orange song
Of the dawn-orange finch
In the dawn-orange elm.

There were many Caesars; there was one
Sappho with her lyre in her fingers,
Sappho with her pen in her fingers.

The willow strings of gold
Are gold against a sky of lead,
A gray-haired sky as oppressive as my father
Zeus. The strings shine gold against a sky
Of lapis lazuli. Where is the sky
Most blue? Where is the most acute
Blue, blue note of the curving lyre?
Why should the sky curve in upon us, pressing
Us back as our song expands, ascends,
Peers down?

      Factories stand in the field.
Machines are busy making bread.
I am hungry. I reach out my hand.
How can you hear me above the machines?
I sing, I write, I cry.
Can you follow my tune,
Can you recognize my hand,
            Can

Can you hear me, Mother?
The alders gleam with bronze and gold.
As yet no narcissus is in flower.

5. Helicon

The Eleusinian solution,
A twofold proposal —
For the individual, personal life after personal death,
For the community, impersonal rhythms of impersonal ever-reliving
Nature, both now in doubt,
The one through progressive enfeeblement in the gods,
The other (this diagnosis is only too well known) through man's
Mad magical stretching of his long potent-impotent arms —
Did not of necessity directly affect
Artists qua artists, who went on adoring
Beauty or fame or excitement or joy
Or some other madness of their own.

And if
Beauty has faded with the gods
And must no longer be invoked
Or even named (if merely a mouthing
Of the appellation makes us blush), and fame
Will have nothing more to reflect it — no long
Capitol steps, bright dome, clear pool —
Will have nothing more to outlast — no statue,
No pyramid, no aquilonian wind — and pure
Joy apprehends the shadows
Of gaunt arms like bare branches
Clutching and crashing across
The continents, shall singing stop

Or shall some squatters under the mountain
Practice their tunes in the dark
Just in case a dawn
Should crawl their way, in case
Some listener with hungry ears
Should stumble toward them in that new morning?

Over there, in a corner behind
The black-and-white Baptist steeple
And the low brick gable of the public library,
There through Andrew Carnegie's disinterested generosity,
Rising an orange sun.
Trying to hold open for a moment and another
Sleep-closed, light-delighted eyes.

They were dancing around the violet spring
And around the smoking outdoor altar
Of mighty Zeus, high on the mountain.
The sheep all stopped, and the shepherd, climbing,
Climbed faster to see what could . . . He stopped,
He stepped back. Just barefoot girls,
Dancing in silence around the spring,
Nine, it seemed; but like no girls
Of Ascra or any village or farm
Or town that he knew. They were lithe and tall,
Their long curls glistened, their faces gleamed,
And their violet eyes, when the turns of the dance
Brought each before him, knew him through
And through. And then they began to sing.
No thrush at dawn, no nightingale at dusk,
No flute, no lyre, no selected choir
Would match or mimic those sounds — each voice,
Each note, each chord, each phrase, each tune,
Perfect, and the whole, perfection. His ears
Throbbed, his eyes were glazing, he could scarcely
Stand, he could hardly breathe. And then
They began to speak. They spoke to him.
Shepherd, they said, calmly, softly,
Shameful wild thing, belly only,
Dipping like a duck for bread, we can
Always express fiction as fact,
And we can when we want to tell what is true.
Each voice, though soft, though calm, echoed
In his ears. The soft grass yielded to their feet,
The soft, sweet air of morning caught,
                                        Carried,

Carried, passed along their song.
They danced beyond the columbines,
Beyond pale peach and palest purple
Irises edging the clearing, beyond
The laurels, beyond tall firs, through green
And shadow and dark and flicker and back
And a branch bent low to a slim white quest
And they turned with the laurel toward where he still stood
And into his shaking hand they set
The singer's staff, and dancing around him
They breathed through his gaping mouth a voice.
Of Zeus our father now you will sing
And of us and our harmonies first and last.
And still the morning was violet and rose.

The oriole's aubade, raying
As bright as his orange self.

On another mountain
Zeus spoke to Mnemosyne. Come,
Memory, to me, to the calling
Sky. Remember
The azure above white Athens,
The jagged stars over Delphi's blackness,
Olympic mists in which the sky
Went down to caress invisible rocks
And raucous tunes of unseen sheep
And the rain-green grass and the rain-gray sea.
Remember the sky as solid,
Motionless, metallic. Remember
The sky of moving parts, the machine
In full operation, the ragged clouds
Like hares, the smoother clouds behind
Like tortoises, the leisured moon,
The wandering stars on their old grand tour,
And the fixed stars, stuck,
Unstuck, and stuck again
                                          Without

Without clogging the parade. I mix
My metaphors. The sky,
Like fire, like frost, transforms
Its tropes as one applies them, slapping
Ferns and palms and hills and stars
Around like paint. Remember
The pigmentation, blue, as cold
As frost, ablaze like flame,
Piling through the miles, dissolving
Into dust, resolving
Into measureless sky. Remember
Thunder above the splitting trees,
Lightning sizzling through the room, raindrops
Nestling in the lilacs, glistening
Like small cupped stars. Do not forget
The age of the light of the stars. We sat
Together on that star's earth when the light
Which touches our eyes now set forth, passed us,
Warmed us as we played on another mountain
Nine thousand years ago, in our first youth.
Come,
Memory, to me, the
Sky.

Zeus shook his thundrous locks. His eyes
Were flashing. Hailstones crashed
On dark-cracked sod. Mnemosyne
Went. And they were born —
Nine healthy daughters. Forget
All your cares — all cares — for a moment. The nine
Immortal sisters come singing. The sky
Turns an echoing blue.

A tête-à-tête with a turtle,
Admiring the bright orange trim
And the black glitter of those eyes in the sun.

Another time Zeus said,
Leto, my love, I'm sick
Of my nagging wife. Let's go off together.
His wife was the queen of the gods, but he
Was the king. They went off together.

The mother, heavy with twins,
Came to Athens: No. Went to Athos: No.
Went to Samos, Scyros, Imbros, Lemnos:
No. No, no, no. She came
To Delos, less than two square miles
Of stone set in the sea.
Delos, will you receive me
For the birth of my son? Goddess,
I am afraid, for they say that Apollo
Will be a haughty god. No place
Will be good enough for his birth. He will
Despise his hometown, stamp his godly
Foot, and I will find
Fish swimming above my mountain.
I promise, the goddess replied,
This place shall be sacred to my son.
His temple will rise here and pilgrims
Come with rich gifts and rich hymns. If you promise,
Delos said, it shall be.

For nine days
Beside the palm tree on the slope of the mountain
She suffered, and on the tenth (you know how it went)
The precocious daughter, born first, assisted
Her mother to bring forth a son. He stood up,
Brushed back his flaxen curls,
Slung on his silver bow,
Took up his gold-keyed lyre,
Thought, and sang — the very lord
Of song.

How shall I hymn you,
All ways well-hymned Apollo?

Shall I watch you descend from the peaks of Olympus,
Your arrows clanging on angry shoulders,
Your coming like night? Shall I watch you sit
On a dune by the sea, and hear the twang
Of your silver bow, and see the mules
Die first, and then the dogs, and then
The heroes? Shall I hear
Cremating pyres, pyre upon pyre?

Shall I watch you ascend Olympus,
Easily climbing through the clouds,
And see the gods all tremble and stand
And your mother unstring your bow and cover
Your quiver and hang your bright weapons on golden
Pegs in your father's golden
Palace and Zeus in welcome
Hand you himself the golden
Cup brimming with golden
Nectar? And shall I watch
You reach for your lyre and pluck the golden
Strings and sing the golden
Songs and lead with high skilled step
The dance of the golden gods?

The papery poppies, orange, far
From sleep, all bright, all orange
Among the purples of the irises.

The first declension: femina, feminae; puella, puellae.
Feminae amicae sunt.

The second declension: vir, viri; puer, pueri.
Viri amici sunt.

The third declension: pater, patris; mater, matris;
Homo, hominis; omnis, omnis; aequalis, aequalis.
Omnes homines aequales sunt.

Once upon a time there was only
The third declension. Mais l'homme,
Hombre, uomo . . . What ever happened
To the good old virile term?
Why on earth was that inhumed?
Man became man. The other?
La belle et la bête.
From man to minx.

Words. Just words, whether just
Or unjust. Let us not fall into a
Decline. Let us arise.
Homo sapiens speaks
No Latin now, for he

Or she or even she or he may speak
A language of minimal inflection

And the aviatrix and the narratrix and the inheritrix
And the actress and the goddess and the heiress
And the authoress and the giantess and the princess
And the stewardess and the murderess and the poetess
Have or will have cut out their tricks
And cut their tresses
And dropped their s's.

How hard it would be
If we spoke Greek.

Le roi est mort. Vive la reine.
Le le est mort. Vive la la.
Over here luckily we have
No royalty, few divinities,
Room for creators and creatrices,
For we hold these truths.

The bride and the bridegroom walk up the aisle.
The man and the wifeman walk down the street.

And life goes along
As the stream beneath monoecious and dioecious trees
And the ducks and the drakes on top of the stream
And the monkeys and apes on top of the trees,
And with much travail the masterpiece is made
And after long labor the mastersinger sings
His song. She sings a mistresssong.

Gazing deep into the deep
Purple of the iris, glinting
Sharp in high noon, soft, deep.

Color into which you gaze —
Not into the iris — into the sheer
Depths of purple, into those depths.

Purple petals lifted,
Purple petals open-armed,
Purple tuneful tongues.

At dusk a purple dark to black.
Behind, rising, white
To purple, whitest purplest white.

Three threes seen,
Dark, centered, deep,
Three purple threes.

Behind the dark the light,
Before the light the dark,
White to purple, purple to black.

One in three threes,
One darkest flower,
Three threes in one.

Flexible, changing, soft,
Strong, unchanged, unconquerable,
Let us say, given the winters.

A dark look, prolonged
In longing, into the heart
Of deep green and purple June.

Father Zeus. Father O'Flaherty.
Father il Papa. Pater noster.
Father George Washington. Uncle Sam.
Uncle Hades. Father Freud.
Pater omnipotens Deus. By Jupiter,

Once there was a father who spun.
He couldn't fix the faucet or a broken doll,
He couldn't drive an auto or a needed nail,
But he could spin. Tell us a story.
You're here. Tell us a story.

I have to get wound up, he would say,
And somehow his daughters devised a plan
Of twisting their fists near his head or his arm.
On the evening of which I speak, he would say,
And then they would not move. Their eyes,
Big, round, almost unblinking, were fixed
Upon the ever-moving thread.

On the evening of which I speak,
Annabel and Isabel were sitting
In the great green chair.

                      From a place like that
Adventure drew through Chew-Gum Forest,
By Lolly-Pop Copse, up Sun-Up Hill,
Where the chugging bus would pass you full
Of all the girls and boys you'd know
In years to come: Elizabeth and John,
Samuel and Virginia, Celeste and Antoine —
This one tall, black-haired, black-eyed,
With a bright green collar; that one, short,
With auburn curls and a pale blue belt.

Patrick and Pericles, the Mischief-Makers,
Would play some tricks, and the Tick-Tock Dogs
Throw motion pictures in your path to lead
Explorers astray.

                But you'd find a friend,
Maybe Philip, though he was very small,
Having been made of the last of the dough
When the Pumpernickels were baked for the tree;
Or Peter, the first to reach up his hands,
Untie the red ribbon, and jump to the floor,
And announce from the middle of the old green rug,
In the middle of the room, in the middle of the building,
In the middle of Chicago, in the middle of America,

That he was Peter Pumpernickel
And had a cousin Lily Pickle
And was made of ginger bread;
He'd a ginger coat and a ginger vest
And he did his ginger, ginger best.

With Peter or Paul or Percival you'd reach —
After wondrous excitements along the way
(To make a short story long, he would say),
Past the Topsy-Turvy House (Which side
Was floor or ceiling, ceiling or floor?) —
The Golden Playground. There the swings
Could swing you anywhere: Denver; California,
Where the mountains come down to the edge of the ocean;
Peking; Moscow; Paris; London;
Bangor, Maine; or Austin, Texas;
Buenos Aires, Argentina;
Resolute; Komsomolets;
Cook Ice Shelf; Dibble Iceberg Tongue.

And then do you know what happened?
O no, O no, the children would cry.
They woke up, he said.

And went on to adventures of their own.
His grave, at his request, read, Penitent.

She must blame the fathers: Father Pacelli,
Father Zeus, and Father O'Malley,
Uncle Dis (polyonymous),
Uncle Sam (pseudonymous),
Founding Father (anonymous),
Jupiter (synonymous);
But that father of joy and adventure
She may not censure.

Irises' various purplings among
The opening strong
Orangenesses of the lilies.

The shepherdess was gathering flowers.
Girls will do that, you know.
Heidi, Europa, Creusa, Persephone,
Flora, all gape and gasp and gaze
After those bits of — what shall I say —
Of color, of odor, of texture, of form,
Those bits of beauty, they might say (poetesses),
Gazing at delphiniums growing toward the blues
Of meridians, gasping at the sunrise —
Orange, yellow, rose — of the snapdragons below them,
Gaping at the quintessential columbines
In fivefoldness, with their comet tails,
Or clematis lit purple on the lamppost,
Or catalpa blossoms bee-sweet on the tree.

She heard a noise among the leaves
By the stream. Black-masked for the ball
The cedar waxwing danced. And masks
Crossed other faces, or should she
Have gouged those pin-prick eye-holes
On her own persona? But her eyes
Were wide open. She looked
Before she leapt.

        Was he a flower?
Or a songbird? Dulcet on the branches?
From which a melody or fragrance reached
Her senses, touched them, took them away?
From her to him? To hues before
Unseen, to notes unheard? Inside
A gray jacket? Under a tan leather
Vest? Under a loud authoritative
Hi? Did sunrise, melodious
In orange and rose, expand
And the snapdragon snap her up?
Was she gone?

        Was he a tree?
To climb as boys climb trees?
Grabbing, holding, hugging, victor?
One with those long arms, with large
Grasping, granting hands? Hands
On her hair, on her shoulders, on her, throbbing
With mighty pulsations, with spring's
New sap, with old
Old tunes?

        Was he a stream?
Filled with clouds and sky? Not the stream
Of February, when solely moving, slowly across the bridge,
Went lengths of train laden from the northern forests? Not the stream
Of reeds and trees rooted in ice? Not the stream
Of ice? A stream with the liquid scent
Of water flowing, the sunny scent
Of grasses growing on the bank, the scent
Of wild sea roses at the edge? A stream
Of the rippling rose of sunset,
The oriole's last flash to the nest
Dangling over the darkening mirror,
The robin's gurgle of goodnight,
The final completorial ripple of the thrush?
A splash — the last flick of a swallow,
Her white breast meeting the dim

                                        Breast

Breast of the water, or was it the moon
In whiter nudity plunging?
And did she throw herself in?

The turtle turned, slid down the stony
Bank, slithered through tall grasses,
Went swimming muddily off. But when
I came back, the turtle was back, a bit upstream,
On the mown grass, taking the sun. I took care
Where I cast my shadow.

                    Or was she accosted,
As one is in summer by fragrances,
By the nine immortal women singing?
Two or three would have been enough,
But nine all going at once
As when you saunter by the stream on an evening
And all the birds are going at once
With a rondo here, a mazurka there,
Here a sonata, there a waltz,
Or basil and garlic and dill,
And broccoli dewy and blue in the garden,
And pineapple woody and leaved on the table.

Hail, O Heliconiades, hail.
What shall I sing?

White, white, white,
The snow, the ash, the bride.

The businesswoman's elegant violet sandals,
The elegant elevation of those elegant slender heels,
Below the slender shapely shaven legs.

Brew, brew, brew,
The brew in the indigo bowls.

Her blue-striped shopping bag lying on the avenue,
The paper in it to be saved,
Not thrown with her into the Hudson River.

The green garland, not of bay —
Of thyme or parsley.

Goldilocks with her broom, sweeping,
Sweeping her way through the kitchen,
Sweeping into the empyrean.

Bathed and veiled, the widow stepping
Proudly into the orange blaze.

Blood, blood, blood,
Coming, coming, coming,
Her bloody red blood.

The sky tonight as echoing the Muses,
Or Muses ever echoing the sky.

The sun set to
The robin's darkening antiphon.

                              Oh,
They bathed in the limpid Permessus.
Their feet felt rocks and leaves and mud.
They bent down and splashed clear water
On smooth breasts and over smooth shoulders
With splashings like song. And no one saw them.

They walked beneath the great elm.
That wasn't hard to see

Between the Doric chapel
And the great Corinthian library.

Obscure Judiths were now permitted
Within the great university.

The elm, though American, not Ionic,
Combined Ionicity of line

And curve with its barbarous exuberance,
Standing there old and young, brown

And green, unmoving and moving,
Mother and maid in one,

Like the strong mother with rough strong hands
That rubbed your blouses on the washboard
And wonderfully rubbed your bed-hot back
And wonderfully summoned strong tones or soft
From the old piano; the same strong mother
With the soft girl's voice that sang
The morning songs, that read
The bedtime stories, the bedtime poems
Whose echoes never ended. You hear them.

The tree in the breeze is a stream or an ocean.
Then are the sparrows sandpipers,
The sociable pigeons seagulls,
These hot stone chapel steps the sand?
One could swim in the waves of the leaves
Or along the current of the trunk.
The leaves look cool like clear green waters.
The ridged brown current looks strong.
It would carry you swiftly away.
It carries you swiftly away
Along its irresistible lines,
Along its total air-bordered form,
Upward, upward, outward, outward,
Away. Where? You're almost there.
Dust blows. A city stands on this shore.
And the leaves? If you dive into the leaves
They are waves and particles, going and remaining,
Waves of music not subject to time
All summer. Do you prefer
This then to a genuine ocean —
An ocean tossing its leaves
Like a great blue tree?
                        From below,
In the shade of the afternoon current,
Under the sun-soaked waves,
You find cool green light coming through.

You find not merely form,
Not merely pure form of desire,
But useful things: oxygen, shade,
Ecstasy, strength, escape, relief.

                              Oh,
They walked by the lingering Messalonskee.
She certainly saw them there.
The still brown stream was a long, long trunk.
At the little dam was a swish as of leaves.
Clear song rippled clear air.

Below stern pines and breezy willows
A moon crouched in the mud.
Above, in orange plenitude a moon
Stepped shimmering.

                      Walk with me, moon,
Beside neat blue luxuriance of spruces,
Beside wild silvery luxury of maples,
Beside smooth coppery lushness of the maples,
Beside amplitudinous greenery of this maple,
And stop by the steeple.
Bold, you remain in the open,
While I, half domestic, climb up the bank,
Obscured on the mud like a slumbering duck,
But I do not sleep, I possess the moon,
She said, or its bright companionship,
Or am possessed. It dazzles now
And now transforms an island cloud
Into a habitable desert. And now
The clouds go, and the steeple and the tree
And the nighthawk, shouting, shooting, and the cat
And I and the moon possess the night.

Is possession equal to desire?
Form is that desire,
Felt and found and formed,
Informed, deformed, reformed, then
Felt and found and formed again,
Like frost, like fire,
Like waters cooled and pavements warmed,
Like something almost possessed,
Restful and never at rest.

The Gardens of Flora Baum

Set in 11-point Scala OT, the Open Type
version of the typeface created in
1990 by Dutch type designer
Martin Majoor and first
used for printing
programs at
Vredenburg Music
Centre, Utrecht. The name
honors Milan's La Scala opera house.

Printing: Lulu.com

Book design: Roger Sinnott